Trade Through the Himalayas

TRADE
THROUGH THE
HIMALAYAS

*The Early British Attempts
to Open Tibet*

By

SCHUYLER CAMMANN

GREENWOOD PRESS, PUBLISHERS
WESTPORT, CONNECTICUT

TO MY PARENTS

INTRODUCTION

THE story of the early English attempts to open Tibet is an interesting one from several points of view. It deals with some little-known activities of the East India Company regarding trans-Himalayan trade, which, when discussed at all, have usually been misrepresented. It shows the eager, commercial-minded diplomacy of the eighteenth century English Company members opposed to the rather suspicious, theocratic feudal spirit of the Tibetans of that time, the equally suspicious feeling of the rulers of the smaller Himalayan countries, and the jealousy of the expanding Manchu Empire of China. Even more important, from the point of view of diplomatic history, these events form the background for the later, better-known British efforts to open Tibet in the late nineteenth and early twentieth centuries. Without a clear picture of the earlier period, and some understanding of the attitudes of the various parties involved—English, Tibetan, Chinese, Bhutanese, and Nepalese—at the time of their first contacts, it is impossible to understand fully why these various people acted as they did in the later situations.

The writer became interested in this phase of British and Asiatic history after various travels in the Tibetan borderlands of West China and Northern India, and several years of research in Tibetan history, culture, and religion. In the course of these investigations, it became clear that there was much confusion in the accounts of the first contacts between the English and the Tibetans, and until this was straightened out, many of the later events would be more or less incomprehensible.

The chief primary sources on the English side were the travel journals of Bogle and Turner and Kirkpatrick, all three long out of print. And in spite of Sir Clements Markham's efforts to edit Bogle's papers almost a hundred years after they were first written, the works of the three men have never been properly synchronized and correlated with each other, much less with material from Asiatic sources. Under the latter heading come the Chinese accounts in the Ch'ing Dynastic records, and the very brief references to the English missions in the Tibetan biographies of the Panchen Lamas, which have recently been discovered.

In this situation, it seemed that a more thorough study of the period would not only be helpful for the writer's own studies, but would also be of value to historians who might want verified facts on this period. The original monograph that resulted from this project formed the writer's Ph.D. thesis at Johns Hopkins University, but it has since been extensively revised in the light of further research. Parts of Chapter III have appeared in an article in the *Far Eastern Quarterly*.

The advice and encouragement of Professor Owen Lattimore have been invaluable, and without the assistance of Mortimer Graves and the American Council of Learned Societies this project could not have been undertaken. Thanks are also due to the staff of the Library of Congress, particularly to Dr. Arthur Hummel of the Division of Orientalia, Colonel Willard Webb who kindly arranged special facilities for research, and Mr. B. H. Brown. The maps drawn by Mrs. C. S. Coon are gratefully acknowledged, along with the fine photographs lent by Colonel C. S. Cutting. Last but not least, the writer's wife Marcia de F. Cammann also deserves much gratitude for her helpful suggestions and assistance.

SCHUYLER CAMMANN

Philadelphia, 1950.

CONTENTS

INTRODUCTION   vii

CHAPTER I. Historical Background: Tibet until 1774.   3

CHAPTER II. The First English Mission to Tibet, 1774-1775.   27

CHAPTER III. Bogle's Report on Tibetan Trade; Sequels to his Mission.   54

CHAPTER IV. Samuel Turner's Mission to Tibet in 1783.   82

CHAPTER V. The Background of the Sino-Nepalese War.   102

CHAPTER VI. The Chinese Campaign Against the Gurkhas, and its Aftermath.   121

CHAPTER VII. Conclusion.   144

APPENDIX A. The Preliminaries to the Bhutan Expedition of 1773.   155

APPENDIX B. The Panchen Lama's First Letter to Warren Hastings.   157

APPENDIX C. The Principal Articles of the Treaty of Peace with Bhutan in 1774.   160

APPENDIX D. Summary of Turner's list of Articles in the Tibetan Trade in 1782.   162

BIBLIOGRAPHY: The Principal Works Cited.   165

INDEX   181

ix

ILLUSTRATIONS

The Manchu Empire and India in the Later
Eighteenth Century   13

Places Involved in Early British Efforts to Open
Tibet   25

The Sixth Panchen Lama   68

The Town of Shigatse   100

Tashilhunpo Monastery   116

x

Trade Through the Himalayas

CHAPTER I

HISTORICAL BACKGROUND: TIBET
UNTIL 1774

TIBET, geographically, is a high plateau in the center of Asia. It consists of rather bleak and barren wastes, cut here and there by mountain chains in which are fertile valleys, and surrounded by the highest ranges in the world. Considered from this point of view, Tibet stretches from Kashmir to Western China, comprising the modern Chinese province of Sikang, and most of Ch'ing-hai (Kokonor), in addition to what is marked on our present-day maps as "Tibet."

Culturally, Tibet includes parts of the Chinese provinces of Szechuan, Kansu, Yunnan, and Ladakh, part of Western Tibet, which has been ruled by Kashmir for about a century. However, the peoples of this vast area belong to several races, and have many individual differences in language, dress and customs, within the common culture.

Historically, Tibet has also on occasion ruled, and long influenced, the frontier states of Nepal, Sikkim, and Bhutan on the southern slopes of the Himalayas, which in the last century came under British control.

Thus we see that geographical Tibet, cultural Tibet, and historical Tibet are overlapping areas with a common core—the "Tibet" of our maps—which might be described as "political Tibet." During the past two centuries, when external aggressors have been hacking away at the peripheral areas, this inner portion has come to be thought of as

"Tibet proper," and people tend to forget the larger entities.

In discussing the historical background of Tibet before the English became interested in it, we shall use the name in its broadest senses; but when we come to consider the English efforts to penetrate "Tibet," we shall have to use it in its narrowest sense of "political Tibet," for this is what the English officials, historians, and writers had in mind.

The vast height of the fringing ranges, the bleakness of the landscape in general, and the extremes of climate have always made Tibet comparatively inaccessible to outsiders.[1] In addition, the peoples of Tibet have—fairly recently—taken to discouraging all visitors from other countries, with a few exceptions, such as their coreligionists from Mongolia and China. Thus it has come to be called the "Forbidden Land." The country has not always been so closed to outsiders, however. We shall see, in briefly tracing its history, that for many years it was open to external influences, through trade and other contacts, particularly from India, Mongolia, and China.

The inhospitable physical features of Tibet which discouraged invaders, conversely caused it to become a refuge area for peoples of various races since the dawn of history; though not all of these were refugees in the usual sense of the word.[2] Until the seventh century A.D., it was just a territory of scattered tribes, and the peoples of Tibet were unable to form a nation. For many centuries before their unification, however, the "Tibetan" peoples on China's

[1] The best short account of the geography of Tibet and its influence on the peoples of that country is given by the late Sir Charles Bell, in *The People of Tibet* (Oxford, 1928), Chapter 1. A very detailed account of the subject, old but still valid, is found in C. R. Markham's *Narratives of the Mission of George Bogle to Tibet and the Journey of Thomas Manning to Lhasa*, 2nd ed. (London, 1879), Introduction, pp xxiii-xlii.

[2] See Lattimore, *Inner Asian Frontiers of China* (New York, 1940), pp. 209-11.

western frontiers had been strong enough to constitute a considerable nuisance.[3] But in their contacts with the Chinese through frontier raids and border trade, these proto-Tibetans apparently did not acquire any Chinese civilization to speak of. The History of the T'ang Dynasty (A.D. 618-907), describes them as they appeared at the time of the first diplomatic contacts in the seventh century, as a people generally nomadic, who kept records with notched sticks and knotted cords, and on occasion practiced human sacrifice.[4]

The unification was accomplished under a king named Song-tsan Gam-po,[5] who is believed to have come from Ladakh, in the far western corner of Tibet, where Indian civilization could have penetrated by way of the Indus Valley.[6] In 634, soon after the founding of the new nation with its capital at Lhasa, in Central Tibet, Song-tsan Gam-po entered into diplomatic relations with the Chinese court, and asked for one of the Emperor's daughters in marriage. When the T'ang Emperor refused the request, the Tibetans invaded West China, and seven years later

[3] Owen Lattimore points out that the Chinese themselves brought about this situation. *Ibid.*, p. 509.

[4] *Chiu T'ang-shu*, 196 (1). 1b-2. The passages relating to Tibet in the T'ang History have been translated by S. W. Bushell, in "The early history of Tibet from Chinese sources," *Journal of the Royal Asiatic Society*, XII (London, 1880), 435-541. (Hereafter the title of this journal will be abbreviated as *JRAS*.)

[5] His name is spelled in Tibetan Srong-btsan sGam-po, but in rendering this and other Tibetan names, we are giving the phonetic simplifications, omitting the letters usually not pronounced. His life, from Tibetan sources, is found in W. W. Rockhill, *The Life of the Buddha* (London, 1884), pp. 211-15, and from Chinese sources, in Bushell, *ibid.*, pp. 443-46. Bushell speaks of him as "Lungtsan," deriving this from the second half of the Chinese transcription of his name.

[6] See Rev. A. H. Francke, "The kingdom of gNya-khri-btsanpo, the first king of Tibet," *Journal and Proceedings of the Asiatic Society of Bengal*, VI (Calcutta, 1910), 93-99. The author convincingly shows, on philological grounds, that the history of "Tibet" before the time of Song-tsan Gam-po, as presented in the Tibetan chronicles, must deal with a petty kingdom in what is now Ladakh, and does not apply to Tibet proper.

their king received a Chinese princess.[7] Princess Wên-ch'êng, who appears to have been a remarkable woman, joined with the king's other wife, a princess from Nepal, in exciting his interest in Buddhism. They were so successful that the Tibetans later canonized him, and the national literature emphasizes his saintliness, even crediting him with having translated several Buddhist works. However, the T'ang history shows quite clearly that he was more at home on the battlefield.[8] Ultimately the Buddhist religion did tame the warlike spirit of the Tibetans, but before this happened they had overrun Nepal, Northern India, and parts of Turkestan, and had even sacked the capital of China, which had been weakened by civil war (in 763).[9]

The chronicles of Song-tsan Gam-po's reign and those of his successors are largely concerned with the development of Tibetan Buddhism, and tend to neglect the secular aspects of the nation's growth.[10] This is partly because, as Sir Charles Bell remarks, "history, unless it centers on religion, does not appeal to the Tibetan mind";[11] this in turn is explained by the fact that Tibetan Buddhism was the principal unifying force that held together a nation of many diverse peoples with individual local cultures. It

[7] Rockhill, *Life of the Buddha*, p. 213.

[8] Bushell, *ibid.*, pp. 443-46. Though Song-tsan Gam-po is even credited with having translated several Buddhist works (Rockhill, *ibid.*, p. 212), Waddell, the great authority on Tibetan Buddhism, tends to minimize this king's contributions to the spread of the faith. See L. A. Waddell, *The Buddhism of Tibet, or Lamaism*, 2nd ed. (Cambridge, 1939), pp. 22-23. (Hereafter we shall refer to this important work by its customary abbreviation, *Lamaism*.)

[9] See C. P. Fitzgerald, *China, a Short Cultural History* (New York and London, 1938), p. 299.

[10] See Sarat Chandra Das, "Contributions on Tibet," *Journal of the Asiatic Society of Bengal*, L, (Calcutta, 1881), Pt. 1, pp. 218-30. (In future references to this journal we shall use the usual abbreviation *JASB*.)

[11] Sir Charles Bell, *Tibet, Past and Present* (Oxford, 1924), p. 23. See also his comments on Tibetan historical works, *ibid.*, p. 22.

was, and is, the one element in their national life that all "Tibetans" have shared in common, to a greater or less degree.

Tibetan Buddhism gradually came to assume a very distinctive form which we know as Lamaism.[12] This was a fusion of the late, rather debased Buddhism of Northern India, and the indigenous Bön religion, accomplished in the latter part of the eighth century through the aid of a missionary from India named Padma Sambhava.[13] He made a lasting impression on the Tibetans by his use of magic and sorcery, and gained many followers who helped him to build monasteries and temples as centers for the new faith.

These monasteries became centers of a Lamaist culture, which increased in complexity as it borrowed elements from other religions such as Manichaeism and Nestorian Christianity. In its secular aspects it was equally eclectic, taking freely from both China and India, and yet it managed to adapt the borrowings without mere slavish imitation. For example, the alphabet invented for transscribing the Buddhist scriptures into Tibetan was based on an Indian script,[14] although the Tibetan language is like Chinese in being built up from monosyllabic elements. The calendar, though built on an Indian model, agrees more or less with the Chinese system of reckoning time, and uses terms borrowed from the Chinese but expressed in Tibetan. The architecture appears to have been based on an early Near Eastern form of construction which did

---

[12] The term Lamaism is an artificial foreign expression. The Tibetans themselves have no special name for their particular form of Buddhism. The word is derived from the Tibetan title *bLa-ma*, which is properly held only by the heads of monasteries or by monks of the highest orders, but is now used by courtesy in referring to almost all monks and priests in Tibet and Mongolia. It means "the Superior One." See Waddell, *Lamaism*, pp. 28-29.

[13] *Ibid.*, pp. 24-28.

[14] For the theory that the Tibetan script was developed in Turkestan, see Francke, "Kingdom," pp. 97-98.

not have the arch;[15] yet many lama temples have columns and doorways of Indian style and Chinese-type roofs. The arts, in particular, demonstrate the ability of the Tibetans to assimilate foreign elements and create distinctive new forms of considerable merit.[16]

The religion introduced by Padma Sambhava had in it, however, many elements of corruption, in addition to its reliance on magic and demon worship (the latter resulting from a compromise with the old Bön faith). This was especially manifest in the emphasis on sexual elements. The later Buddhism of Northern India, to which Padma Sambhava and his Indian missionary successors subscribed, put considerable stress on the philosophic concept of the union between the spiritual and material forces in the universe. It represented this by paintings and images showing the physical union of god and goddess,[17] and practiced and encouraged sexual excesses as a form of worship.[18] This aspect of the Indian faith took a firm hold on the Tibetan

[15] Many examples of this type of architecture are found in the Hadramaut region of Southern Arabia, and the type extends as far west as the Atlas Mountains of North Africa. Compare the photographs in Freya Stark's *Seen in the Hadramaut* (New York, 1939), facing pp. 18, 21, 25, 48, etc., and S. Sitwell's *Mauretania* (London, 1940), p. 142, with Marco Pallis' *Peaks and Lamas* (London and Toronto, 1939), frontispiece.

[16] See S. Cammann, "The Paradise of Bhaisajyaguru," *Gazette des Beaux Arts*, 6th series, xxv (1944), 283-98, for pictures of several types of Tibetan paintings and a discussion of the tradition behind Lamaist painting in general.

[17] For examples, see F. Lessing, *Yung-ho-kung* (Stockholm, 1942), pl. xxv, and Alice Getty, *The Gods of Northern Buddhism* (Oxford, 1914), pls. XLIV and XLV. The concept of unity in duality (less physically expressed), together with the contrary one of two basic elements in opposition, runs all through Eastern Asiatic philosophy and permeates the arts and daily life. For a more sophisticated expression of this concept, see S. Cammann, "A Rare T'ang Mirror," *The Art Quarterly*, IX (1946), 93-114.

[18] These particular elements, and related ones, found in later Indian Buddhism may not have been indigenous, but rather introduced from China, where they had long played an important part in the early Taoist faith. See S. Cammann, "Suggested Origin of the Tibetan Mandala Paintings," *The Art Quarterly*, XIII (1950), 107-119.

mind, and has tended to nourish unhealthy minds among the predominantly ignorant lamas. The monks of the older (Red) sects of Lamaism were rarely celibate, and have frequently had wives or concubines, but the lamas in general have been, and are, notorious for their licentiousness.[19] Rare is the monk who can see beyond the very graphically portrayed images to perceive the doctrine of the ultimate union of the soul with the Infinite. And rare is the one who can admit that the numerous Buddhas, bodhisattvas, goddesses and even demons, are only manifestations of the one Supreme Being in his various aspects, and that the specific approach to Him through one or another deity does not much matter. The majority are extremely literal-minded.[20]

From time to time, however, these deeper teachings of philosophic Buddhism were revived by teachers from India. The greatest of these was Atisha, who came to Tibet in the eleventh century, and succeeded in instituting important reforms.[21] Meanwhile Tibetan monks often went down into India to visit the holy places of Buddhism, and maintained close contact with the Indian monasteries in Bengal.[22] At the end of the twelfth century, however, the Moslems conquered northeastern India, destroying the Buddhist religion there,[23] and as a result later influences on Tibetan culture tended to come from China.

Diplomatic relations with China, which had been broken

19 *Lamaism*, pp. 74-75.

20 For some typical beliefs and practices of popular Lamaism, see S. Cammann, "Glimpses of the Lama religion in Tibet and Mongolia," *University Museum Bulletin*, xiv (August, 1949), 3-32.

21 *Lamaism*, pp. 35-36, text and notes.

22 Markham, *Narratives*, pp. 196-97.

23 Vincent Smith, in *The Oxford History of India*, 2nd ed. (Oxford, 1928), p. 221, says the Muhammedan conquest of Bengal took place about the end of the year 1199. *The Cambridge History of India* (Cambridge, 1928), iii, 46, says it took place in 1202. We accept the first date, since it is the one generally cited, and because Vincent Smith has a reputation for care and accuracy.

soon after their inception in the T'ang period, were resumed during the Yüan or Mongol dynasty, when Khubilai Khan favored Lamaism as the state religion of his empire. Towards the close of the thirteenth century, this powerful sovereign invested the current head of the dominant Lamaist sect (Sa-kya) with a title and seal which implied that he was the ruler of Tibet, thus inaugurating the long tradition of theocratic rule.[24]

Shortly after the end of the Yüan dynasty, a new reformer arose on the China side of Tibet. This was Tsong Ka-pa who led the followers of Atisha to form a new sect, called the *Gelug-pa* or Yellow Caps,[25] whose members wore yellow hats to distinguish them from the older sects which wore red. This sect rapidly assumed the position of dominance once held by the Sa-kya lamas, not only in religion but in politics as well. It owed its political rise to the patronage of various Mongol rulers, who played it off against the firmly entrenched, and numerically more powerful, Redcap sects; although some of the Mongol princes, conversely, took the side of the older sects in persecuting the Yellow Caps when it seemed politically expedient to do so.[26]

This important development took place after the reconversion of the Mongols to Lamaism in the latter half of the sixteenth century. The chief agent in winning over the Mongols was Tsong Ka-pa's fourth successor as head of the Yellow Church, and in return, he was awarded the title of "Dalai Lama Vajradhara" by Altan Khan of the Tumets.[27] (The title of Dalai Lama was granted posthu-

[24] Cf. Waddell, *Lamaism*, pp. 37-38, also W. W. Rockhill, *The Dalai Lamas of Lhasa and their relations with the Manchu emperors of China* (Leyden, 1910), p. 2.

[25] Waddell, *Lamaism*, pp. 58-63.

[26] See Sarat Chandra Das, "Tibet under her last kings (1434-1642)," and "Tibet a dependency of Mongolia (1643-1716)," *JASB*, new ser., I (1905), 165-67, 152-55, respectively.

[27] Rockhill, *Dalai Lamas* (Leyden, 1910), pp. 4-5.

mously to his two predecessors, so he is officially recognized as the "Third Dalai Lama."[28])

In spite of the prestige given to the new supreme lama by the patronage of this mighty Mongol prince, however, he did not have the power that had been held by Khubilai Khan's protégé. The head of the Yellow sect did not become in fact the sovereign of Tibet, ruling from Lhasa, until the middle of the seventeenth century, when Gushi Khan of the Oelots conquered Tibet, breaking the power of the Red sects, and handed it over to the Fifth Dalai Lama.[29] At the same time Gushi made one of his sons "King of Tibet," but he did this with the understanding that the latter was to be subordinate to the Dalai Lama. It was this Fifth Dalai Lama, one of the most capable rulers of his time, who began the erection of the Potala Palace on the hill west of Lhasa.[30] This startlingly modern looking building represents the highest achievement of Tibetan architecture, and is one of the wonders of the world.[31]

The Fifth Dalai Lama, shortly before his accession to supreme power honored his old teacher, and the latter's three predecessors, with the title of "Panchen Rinpoche."[32] The title carried with it theoretical control over Further Tibet, which the Panchen was to rule from Tashilhunpo, a great monastery, west of Lhasa.[33] From this time on,

[28] Waddell (*Lamaism*, p. 39) says that the "Fifth Dalai Lama" was the first to receive the title, and his statement has misled later writers. Apparently he based it on an ambiguous remark by Sarat Chandra Das ("Contributions," *JASB*, LI [1882], 27). However, he also refers to C. F. Koeppen, *Die Religion des Buddha*, II (Berlin, 1859), and if he had consulted the proper page of this work (p. 139), he would have seen that the title was indeed conferred on the "Third Dalai Lama."

[29] Rockhill, *Dalai Lamas*, pp. 7-8.   [30] *Ibid.*, p. 8.

[31] Among the best pictures of the Potala at Lhasa are those shown on the cover of *Asia*, XXXIX, no. 3 (March, 1939), and in *Tibet Past and Present*, facing p. 3.

[32] Rockhill, *Dalai Lamas*, pp. 8-9.

[33] In Tibetan spelling, this name appears as bKra-shis lhun-po. Further Tibet, of which Tashilhunpo is the capital, is known as the province of Tsang, as opposed to Central Tibet, the province of U, of which Lhasa

save for occasional interruptions during minorities, or at periods of foreign influence from Mongolia or China, the Dalai and Panchen Lamas shared the rule of Tibet, their successors being considered merely as reincarnations of the same two persons.[34]

Even before the Manchus conquered China in 1644, relations were opened between the Dalai and Panchen Lamas and the Manchu "Emperor," and emissaries from Tibet came to the Manchu court at Mukden in 1642.[35] Ten years later, the Fifth Dalai Lama came personally to China to visit the new Manchu Emperor who was now established in Peking.[36] Some accounts state that the Dalai Lama made this trip in order to recognize in person the suzerainty of the new emperor.[37] But Rockhill, the noted American dip-

---

is the capital. Nearer Tibet, more commonly called Eastern Tibet, is the province of Kham. The last has been partially incorporated into China under the name of Sikang (literally: "Kham in the West").

[34] The theory of reincarnated holy men is a late development of Lamaism, and is definitely not the same as the Hindu-Buddhist theory of reincarnation, though it is an outgrowth from that. See Baron A. von Staël-Holstein, "Notes on two Lama paintings," *Journal of the American Oriental Society,* LII (1932), 338. Waddell asserted that the fully developed Lamaist theory was probably an invention of the Fifth Dalai Lama (*Lamaism,* pp. 230-31); but his reasoning seems largely based on his false assumption that the Fifth Dalai Lama was the first to bear this title (see note 28 above).

[35] Later historians seem to disagree on who made the first overtures. The *Ch'ing-shih kao* (1928), 530.2b, basing its testimony on official documents, states that the Manchu court first sent messengers to the Dalai Lama and the temporal king of Tibet (Gushi Khan's son) in 1639, whereupon the Dalai and Panchen Lamas sent an embassy back. The *Shêng wu chi,* by Wei Yüan (1842), states that a mission from the Dalai and Panchen Lamas, Gushi Khan, and the King of Tibet, arrived at Mukden, the Manchu capital, with letters and presents in 1642, and that letters were sent back in the following year (1643), marking the beginning of relations between Tibet and the Ch'ing Dynasty (*op.cit.,* 5.4). Rockhill (*Dalai Lamas,* pp. 9-13) tries to reconcile the two traditions, but has miscalculated the dates, stating that the mission from Tibet arrived at Mukden in 1643 and left in 1644.

[36] Rockhill, *ibid.,* pp. 16-18.

[37] *Eminent Chinese of the Ch'ing Dynasty,* ed. by A. W. Hummel (1943-1944), p. 256.

lomat and scholar, wrote of this visit,[38] that the Dalai
Lama had been treated with all the ceremony that could
have been accorded to any independent sovereign, and
nothing can be found in Chinese works to indicate that he
was looked upon in any other light; for at this period of
China's relations with Tibet, it cannot be denied that the
temporal power of the Lama, backed by the arms of Gushi
Khan and the devotion of other Mongol tribes was not a
thing for the Emperor of China to question—especially as
his dynasty was new and still insecure.

The manner of the Dalai Lama's reception alone, is not
sufficient evidence that he was considered as an independent
sovereign. For we shall see in Chapter III that a later
Panchen Lama was received in Peking with fully as much
pomp, when both host and guest were well aware that the
Lama was merely a vassal, though a powerful one. But
in this early period of its rule, the Manchu Government
apparently did not yet claim any real sovereignty over
Tibet.

In fact, as Rockhill further points out, previous dynasties in China never had any political control over Tibet.[39]
During the T'ang Dynasty the Tibetans were at least
military equals of the Chinese, and the isolationist Sung
Dynasty never even encouraged diplomatic relations with
the Tibetans. The Mongol Dynasty's claim to a vague
suzerainty over Tibet was apparently based solely on the
relations between the Sa-kya Grand Lamas and Khubilai

[38] Rockhill, *Dalai Lamas*, p. 18.
[39] *Ibid.*, p. 3. Modern Chinese Nationalism, of course, has a very
different line. It is claimed that the allegiance of Tibet to China dates
back to the Sui and T'ang dynasties, that in the Yüan, or Mongol, dynasty,
the administration of Tibet was in the hands of one department of the
Imperial government, and that over thirteen hundred years have elapsed
since Tibet first acknowledged its allegiance to China—the implication
being that there has been no break since. (See for example Chiang Kai-
shek, *China's Destiny*, authorized ed. [New York, 1947], p. 11.) This
represents an unwarranted juggling of historical facts for imperialistic
ends.

The Manchu Empire and I

URGA

MONGOLIA

JEHOL

PEKING

MANCHURIA

KOREA

SINING
KANSU
MBUM

SZECHUAN

CHINA

HAM
CHIENLU

YUNNAN

CANTON

ANNAM

SIAM

South

China

Sea

CAM-
BODIA

0   500   1000
MILES

The Later Eighteenth Century

Khan and his successors. But this was a purely nominal bond. In spite of Marco Polo's implications to the contrary, the Mongol armies never penetrated Tibet proper,[40] and even though their dynasty is supposed to have divided the country into administrative districts like those of China (*chün* and *hsien*),[41] this seems to have been merely a paper creation, not carried out in fact. Later emperors of the Mongol and Ming dynasties sent titles, seals of office, and rich gifts to high lamas and chieftains in Tibet,[42] in return for presents and trade goods which the latter sent on so-called "tribute missions";[43] but relations stopped there. The emperors in question never established any actual domination over the temporal rulers of Tibet the way the Mongol princes did in the seventeenth century.[44]

It would seem that the Manchus, quite early in their empire-building career, had in mind the possibility of extending their rule over Tibet. For in 1657 the Court approved a suggestion that each Banner (military division of the Manchus) should select men to learn the written language of Tibet.[45] A policy of Tibetan conquest emerged more strongly in the reign of the second great Manchu ruler of China, the K'ang-hsi Emperor (1662-1721). He apparently considered it for some time, as shown by his

[40] Marco Polo, describing "the province of Tebet," speaks of territory sorely ravaged in the wars of Mangu Khan (Khubilai's brother). See *The Book of Ser Marco Polo*, ed. by Colonel Henry Yule (London, 1871), II, 26. But Yule points out that the Venetian was referring to what is now Western Szechuan and Yunnan, and not to Tibet proper or even Eastern Tibet (*ibid.*, p. 29, note 1).

[41] *Ta-Ch'ing i-t'ung-chih*, 352.1b.

[42] *Ibid.*, pp. 1b-2, and *Shêng wu chi*, 5.2-4.

[43] For the true role of the "tribute missions," and their significance in the trade of Imperial China, see Fairbank and Têng, "On the Ch'ing tributary system," *Harvard Journal of Asiatic Studies*, VI (1941), pp. 135-41.

[44] Rockhill (*Dalai Lamas*, p. 3) states dogmatically that there is not a single reference in the histories of the Yüan and Ming dynasties to political relations having been established at any time with the temporal rulers of Tibet.

[45] Kuang-hsü *Hui-tien shih-li*, 992.14b.

gracious attitude toward the Lama hierarchy, whom he must have inwardly despised to judge from his public comments on the defects of the Buddhist religion.[46] But control over the Lama hierarchy was a necessary step in the Manchu policy of subduing and controlling the Mongols. For many years, however, the Emperor was too occupied with political problems in Mongolia itself to do anything very active about Tibet; although in the meantime, according to Chinese accounts, the high Lamas of Lhasa were giving him plenty of provocation by intriguing with his Mongol enemies.[47]

In 1700, his armies finally took permanent possession of Tachienlu, the gateway to Eastern Tibet, and the key to the road from Szechuan to Lhasa.[48] Eight years later, complaints reached Peking that Latsan Khan, the Mongol temporal King of Tibet, had enthroned a puppet Dalai Lama, and the Emperor sent a commission under a high Manchu official to Lhasa to investigate the situation. As a result of their report of Latsan Khan's difficulties, in the following year (1709), the Emperor sent a still higher Manchu official to Lhasa to assist the King. This step marks the beginning of direct Chinese intervention in Tibetan affairs.[49]

Many of the Mongols objected to the idea of a puppet head of the Yellow Church and a King of Tibet who was supported by the Emperor of China. Accordingly in 1717, an army of Jungars, Oelot Mongols from Turkestan, in-

46 Ernest Ludwig, the German orientalist, points out that the "Sacred Edict" of the K'ang-hsi Emperor sarcastically emphasizes those defects of Buddhism which must have been conspicuous to every mind trained in the spirit of Chinese classics. See E. Ludwig, *The Visit of the Teshoo Lama to Peking* (Peking, 1904), p. 33.

47 Rockhill, *Dalai Lamas*, pp. 19-20, 23-24.

48 *Hsi-tsang t'u-shih* (1792), 1.10b.

49 Rockhill, *Dalai Lamas*, pp. 36-37. An official Court report of March 8th, 1709, gives the findings of the commission and announces the appointment of the Manchu official Ho-shou to go to Lhasa (*Tung-hua ch'üan-lu*, K'ang-hsi, 83.6-6b).

vaded Tibet with the avowed intention of replacing the puppet Dalai with the "true" incarnation.[50] They killed Latsan Khan, deposed the puppet, and then proceeded to ravage the temples and homes in Lhasa, including even the Potala Palace of the Dalai Lamas.[51] This was far worse than the familiar, recurrent Mongol interference in Tibetan affairs, from the Manchu point of view. The Jungars had already attained too much power in Central Asia,[52] and the addition of Tibet to their domain might make them strong enough to found a new Mongol Empire, which could challenge the Manchus and invade China.[53] This was a fine opportunity to chasten the Oelots and at the same time extend the Manchu power over Tibet.

A first army sent from China was badly defeated in the Tibetan highlands by a combined army of Mongols and Tibetans, but the Emperor persisted, sending two more in 1720.[54] These succeeded in capturing Lhasa, conquering Tibet, and driving out the Jungars. This was the first time that an army from China had ever conquered the country; and the victory assured the Manchus of suzerainty over all Tibet, including Bhutan. But even though Tibet had lost her independence, the two Grand Lamas were permitted to retain enormous influence over the nation, temporal as well as spiritual.

Before the punitive armies returned to China, they destroyed the city walls of Lhasa, and on leaving, they left behind a strong garrison. As things seemed quiet in Tibet, the Manchus withdrew their garrison in 1723, and left the Tibetans more or less to themselves; though they erected a stone tablet in Lhasa commemorating their conquest, as

[50] *Eminent Chinese*, p. 908.
[51] These events are graphically described by Fr. Desideri, the Jesuit, who was in Tibet at the time. See Ippolito Desideri, S.J., *An Account of Tibet*, ed. by Filippo de Filippi, revised ed. (London, 1937), pp. 161-62.
[52] See *Eminent Chinese*, p. 758.
[53] See Rockhill's comments on this situation, *Dalai Lamas*, p. 89.
[54] See Desideri, pp. 165-70, and *Eminent Chinese*, p. 908.

a reminder of their power.[55] In 1727, however, a rebellion in Lhasa forced them to take firmer control. They appointed an Imperial Resident and Vice-Resident (called Ambans)[56] to be stationed in the capital; placed the principal districts of Eastern Tibet under the jurisdiction of the provinces of Yunnan and Szechuan; and turned over the temporal government in Lhasa to a loyal chieftain from Further Tibet, whom they made Governor-general with the rank of prince.[57]

All went well in Tibet until 1750, when the Governor-general's son and successor, Gyurmed Namgyal, organized a strong anti-Chinese uprising. He was decoyed into the hands of the Ambans, who killed him. Then they in turn were murdered by a Tibetan mob.[58] As before, this brought a punitive expedition from China which once more conquered Lhasa.[59]

Now the Chinese Government took even sterner measures of control. They reorganized the administration of Tibet, placing four Tibetans of high rank (the Kalons) in charge of civil affairs, instead of entrusting full power to one man. They increased the garrisons in the principal Tibetan towns, and insured open communications between Szechuan and Tibet, via Tachienlu. And finally they made strict rules to prevent the Jungarian Mongols from en-

[55] The text of the inscription on this tablet is given in the Chinese gazetteer of Tibet, *Hsi-tsang chih* (1792), 3.18b-19b, and in Mêng-pao's *Hsi-tsang pei-wên* (1851), pp. 1-2. This inscription is dated 1721; but the date of the erection of the tablet, inscribed on it, is 1724, indicating that is was probably chiseled in China, then transported to Tibet. *Eminent Chinese* (p. 908) states wrongly that it was erected in 1721.

[56] The Residents were traditionally Manchus or Mongols, not Chinese. Their names and dates of office (to 1912) are given in *Ch'ing-shih kao*, chs. 211-14.

[57] See *Eminent Chinese*, pp. 395, 908. The first reference (p. 395) says that the transfer of administration in Eastern Tibet was made in 1725, while the second says that it was done in 1727. The latter date must be correct, because the *Ch'ing-shih kao* (530.7b) and the *Shêng wu chi* (5.13) both discuss the matter under the year 1727.

[58] *Eminent Chinese*, p. 395.   [59] *Ibid.*, p. 250.

tering Tibet again, as they were suspected of instigating the revolt.[60]

From this time on, the influence of China in Tibet became very strong, as the Tibetans now realized that revolts would be speedily and drastically suppressed. However, the Sixth Panchen Lama,[61] after the death of the Dalai in 1757,[62] and during the minority of his reincarnated successor, gained considerable power, which insured his virtually independent control over Further Tibet, at least, until 1779.[63] He was the first Grand Lama to have dealings with the English in India, so we shall have occasion to mention him again.

Meanwhile, Tibet had gradually became known to Europeans. For it certainly is incorrect to say, as did one of Warren Hastings' biographers, that in the mid-eighteenth century, Tibet was a "land of mystery . . . which was not only unknown to the West, but had hitherto been closed to all contact with the West."[64] In 1624 the first Europeans crossed the Himalayas.[65] These were Antonio Andrade and

[60] *Ibid.*, and Rockhill, *Dalai Lamas*, p. 46.

[61] The Sixth Panchen Lama was Lobzang Paldan-yeshes (1738-1780). He is usually miscalled the "third" by Western writers (cf. Waddell, *Lamaism*, p. 236). An abridged version of his Tibetan biography translated into English appears in Sarat Chandra Das, "Contributions," *JASB*, LI (1882) 29-43. This gives a conventionalized portrait of him (pl. XIIIa), but a far better one is shown in *Asia*, XXVI (June, 1929), 476. Another biography of him is given by G. Huth, *Geschichte des Buddhismus in der Mongolei* (Strassburg, 1896), pp. 299-324. This German translation of a Mongol history, also written in Tibetan, is virtually unreadable, because of the great number of Tibetan and Sanskrit terms, and Mongolian and Chinese names in atrocious transcription. The dates for the years are miscalculated one year too early, throughout.

[62] Rockhill (*Dalai Lamas*, p. 46) says that this Dalai Lama died "in 1758, or perhaps a little earlier," and Waddell (*Lamaism*, p. 233) says he died in 1758, but the *Ch'ing-shih kao*, which is generally more reliable than either of these, says that he died in 1757 (*op.cit.*, 530.9b).

[63] Rockhill, *Dalai Lamas*, p. 46, and Markham, *Narratives*, pp. 130-31.

[64] A. M. Davies, *Warren Hastings* (London, 1935), p. 428.

[65] For many years it has been asserted that Father Odoric of Pordenone went to Lhasa in the fourteenth century, and most books on Tibetan exploration have said something to that effect. However, this legend was

Manuel Marques, Portuguese Jesuits, who founded a mission at Tsaparang in Western Tibet.[66] Their mission lasted for a number of years, until the king of that region antagonized the lamas by his favors to the foreign priests.[67] This same pattern was to recur again and again in the history of attempts to open Christian missions in Tibet. In fact, it might be said to have been the typical course of events.[68]

Shortly after, two more Portuguese priests, Frs. Cabral and Cacella, visited Shigatse in Central Tibet, traveling there by way of Bhutan, but the hostility of the lamas prevented them from founding a mission there.[69] Nearly forty years later, in 1661, two more Jesuit missionaries, Frs. Grueber and d'Orville, achieved the remarkable feat of crossing Tibet on their way from China to India.[70] Then, in the first half of the eighteenth century, the Capuchins had a mission in Lhasa itself,[71] and the Jesuit Fr. Desideri came to live there for a number of years, preserving his

---

finally disproved by Berthold Laufer, "Was Odoric of Pordenone ever in Tibet?" *T'oung-Pao*, ser. 2, xv (1914), 405-18. Laufer remarks (p. 416), "It is incredible that he should have traversed Tibet, nor does he himself make any statement to that effect."

[66] See C. Wessels, S.J., *Early Jesuit Travellers in Central Asia 1603-1721* (The Hague, 1924), pp. 43-68.

[67] *Ibid.*, pp. 69-89.

[68] Sir Charles Bell, *The Religion of Tibet* (Oxford, 1931), p. 151.

[69] *Early Jesuit Travellers*, pp. 121-61.

[70] *Ibid.*, pp. 164-202. Fr. d'Orville also used the name de Dorville (*ibid.*, p. 176), and this misled Holdich into stating that de Dorville was apparently his correct name (Col. Sir Thomas Holdich, *Tibet, the Mysterious* [New York, 1906], p. 71).

[71] A general account of the Capuchin Mission is given by Graham Sandberg, *The Exploration of Tibet* (Calcutta and London, 1904), pp. 32-101, and this has been drawn upon by many authors, Bell and Holdich in particular. However, Sandberg's accuracy is so very questionable even when he has used reliable sources, that he is doubly to be doubted when he has relied upon an obscure secondary source, as here (see his note 1, p. 32). R. Orazio della Penna, the leader of the Capuchins in Lhasa, left a short account of Tibet which was published in English by Markham (*Narratives*, pp. 316-40). For some of his other contributions, see P. Frédégand Callaey, "Missionaires capucins et la civilisation thibétaine," *Études Franciscaines*, xlvi (1934), 129-39.

impressions in his remarkable *Account of Tibet*, which has become one of the chief sources for the history of the internal politics of the country at that period.[72] While the Capuchins were there, a remarkable Dutch traveler, Samuel van de Putte, twice passed through the capital on his way from India to China and back again, but unfortunately most of the knowledge he acquired died with him, as he willed that his notes should be destroyed after his death.[73]

In the meantime, in 1717, French geographers in Peking had made a good map of Tibet with information obtained from two lama surveyors whom they had trained for the task.[74] This in turn was published in the famous atlas of Jean Baptiste Bourgignon d'Anville in 1737, and as a result it came to be called "D'Anvilles's map."[75] It was so well done that it was not superseded until the latter part of the nineteenth century.

During this period, a number of books had been published in Europe discussing Tibet from the accounts of missionaries and travelers, the most notable being Giorgi's *Alphabetum Tibetanum*, compiled from materials sent back from Lhasa by the Capuchins.[76] Another was Du Halde's famous *History of China*, in which the author remarked,

[72] See reference in note 51. Fr. Desideri's life is given by Wessels in *Early Jesuit Travellers*, pp. 205-72.

[73] See Markham, *Narratives*, pp. lxii-lxv. The precise dates of his visits to Lhasa are uncertain.

[74] The story of how this map was made is given by Markham, *ibid.*, pp. lxi-lxii.

[75] The map in question is the general map of Tibet, no. 32 in d'Anville's *Nouvel atlas de la Chine, de la Tartarie-chinoise et du Thibet* (The Hague, 1737). Nos. 33-41 in the same volume show details of the area covered in the general map. As late as 1879, Markham stated that this map "still continues to be the basis of our geographical knowledge of (Tibet), although it is rapidly being superseded by the efforts of Colonel Montgomerie and his native explorers."

[76] Published in Rome in 1762. Markham says of Giorgi's book, "The huge work contains a chronology of Tibetan kings and lamas, itineraries, and other information, which is overlaid by a confusing and superfluous mass of erudition and puerile etymologies." (*Narratives*, p. lx, note 2.)

"Though Thibet may be one of the least famous parts of Asia, yet it hath been known for a very long time."[77] In short, Tibet was quite familiar to eighteenth century Europe. But the English had taken no part in its physical and intellectual exploration.

The English East India Company was founded in 1600, and came to India not long after.[78] For a century and a half, however, its representatives apparently did not have the slightest interest in Tibet. They were not particularly moved by the idea of the propagation of faith, as were the Portuguese, or by travel for its own sake. Their primary consideration was trade, and although the English had apparently known about at least one of the commercial possibilities of Tibet—its borax production—since 1644,[79]

[77] J. B. Du Halde, *History of China* (London, 1736), p. 458. This is the English translation of his famous *Description géographique, historique, chronologique, politique, et physique de l'Empire de la Chine et de la Tartarie Chinoise*, first published in Paris, in 1735. The account of Tibet in this work (pp. 441-64) is inclined to be very general, and devotes much space to a discussion of the origin of d'Anville's map of Tibet, since the latter's atlas (see note 75) was composed to accompany this history.

In its general approach, Du Halde's account of Tibet is a great contrast to other geographical books of this period which dealt more with travels in Tibet; such as "Astley's Voyages," *A New General Collection of Voyages and Travels*, actually compiled by John Green, and published by Thomas Astley (London, 1747). The later mentions Fr. Andrade's journeys (with much scepticism), and gives accounts of Grueber's and Desideri's travels in Tibet, closing this section with a description of the founding of the Capuchin mission in Lhasa, and its state in 1741, by della Penna (*ibid.*, IV 649-64). However, "Astley's Voyages" also has a section devoted to a more general account of Tibet (pp. 449-76) which is especially valuable for its bibliographical references to contemporary European books on Tibet and Central Asia in general.

[78] The English East India Company was founded on the last day of 1600. The history of its efforts to gain a foothold in India during the seventeenth century is given in the *Oxford History of India*, pp. 337-41.

[79] A letter to the Company in London from their representatives in India, dated January 27th, 1644, discusses the Company's monopoly on the export of borax, proclaimed in the previous year, and speaks of enclosing particulars concerning its place of origin, which was Tibet;—though the letter does not specifically say so, and unfortunately the enclosure has not been published. See William Foster, *The English Factories in India 1642-1645* (Oxford, 1913), p. 138.

they found enough trade in India itself to satisfy their wants until the second half of the eighteenth century. After they took over Bengal in 1764, however, they soon became interested in the neighboring lands to the north, such as Nepal and Bhutan, wondering what opportunities these offered for trade. Their curiosity even extended further— to Tibet. But they were a little late.

After 1750, circumstances had tended more and more to make Tibet a closed land. First, the assertion of fuller Manchu suzerainty over the country in that year, following the revolt of Gyurmed Namgyal, had strengthened there their imperial policy of seclusion. This policy was no doubt welcome to the lamas, who had apparently been instrumental in the expulsion of the Capuchin missionaries a few years before, and naturally did not welcome further rivals.[80]

Then, the conquest of Nepal by the Gurkhas (completed in 1769),[81] and their replacement of the semi-Tibetan Buddhist culture of the former Newari rulers by a new Hinduized one,[82] tended to shut off the age-old cultural

[80] The expulsion of the Capuchins from Lhasa has long been a subject of controversy. Markham (*Narratives*, p. lxvi) says that they were expelled from Lhasa in about 1760, but gives no reference for that particular date. The Panchen Lama told Bogle in April 1775 that they had been expelled from Lhasa about forty years before (*ibid.*, p. 167), which would have been 1735. Sir Charles Bell dodges the issue, saying that the mission was abandoned in 1745, not from Tibetan opposition, but from lack of funds (*The People of Tibet* [Oxford, 1928], p. 16). Sylvain Lévi, the great French Orientalist, who had access to various Capuchin records in Italian, says that they were expelled by the Chinese in 1745, and states that in that year the Chinese inaugurated the policy of systematic exclusion towards all foreigners in Tibet (*Le Népal* [Paris, 1905] I, 105-6). He is no doubt right about this date, but he says that the Chinese policy followed their suppression of "the uprising of 1736," which is certainly wrong, as there is no record of any Tibetan revolt between 1727 and 1750.

[81] This conquest is described by Lévi, *ibid.*, II, 261-76, and Perceval Landon, *Nepal* (London, 1928) I, 58-66.

[82] An Indian writer, Gaur Das Bysack, describes the Newaris, who ruled Nepal before the Gurkhas conquered it, as an agricultural and commercial race who had borrowed their arts and civilization from Tibet

contacts between Nepal and Tibet, as well as the accustomed avenues of trans-Himalayan trade between Northern India and Tashilhunpo by way of the Nepal passes. Furthermore, the intrigues of the English, in their ineffectual efforts to help the old rulers of Nepal against the Gurkhas, thoroughly annoyed the latter.

In 1767, for example, the English sent an expedition under Captain Kinloch into Nepal against the Gurkhas, and this proved almost totally disastrous to the Company's troops. It succeeded only in arousing the wrath of the Gurkhas at the interference.[83] Two years later, in 1769, Surgeon James Logan was sent on a mission to Nepal in an effort to encourage or support the Newari Rajah of Khatmandu, partly because the latter was believed to be closely connected with the "Pontiff of Lhasa" (the Dalai Lama), and it was hoped that he might be useful in furthering the expansion of trade to Tibet.[84] But this, too, was a failure, for in that year Khatmandu fell to the Gurkhas, who thus completed their conquest of Nepal proper.

Not only did these English efforts fail to help the old rajahs, but they completely alienated the new one. For when the Gurkha chieftain, Prithvi Narayan, took over

---

("Notes on a Buddhist monastery at Bhot Bagan," *JASB* LIX [1890], 59, note 2). Lévi (*Le Népal*, I, 220-21ff.) also attests to their northern origin, in spite of an effort amongst them to claim an Indian heritage. The Gurkhas, on the other hand, stressed their Rajput blood, and emphasized Hindu traditions, though Lévi laughs at their pretensions (*Le Népal*, I, 18, 254).

[83] Lévi, *ibid.*, II, 271, tells how Captain Kinloch's expedition reached Hariharpur, but was obliged to retreat fighting, after swollen streams prevented further advance, and malaria and lack of supplies made it impossible to remain where they were.

[84] See S. C. Sarcar, "Some notes on the intercourse of Bengal with the northern countries in the second half of the eighteenth century," *Bengal: Past and Present* (the journal of the Calcutta Historical Society), XLI (1939), 124-25. This writer included references from a letter sent by Logan to Harry Verelst, Governor of Bengal, preserved in the India Office, Calcutta, as Original Consultation No. 1, of October 31st, 1769, which includes the mention of the possibility for the expansion of the Company's trade to Tibet, referred to in the text above.

Nepal, he did not forget that the English had tried to assist his enemies and block his conquests. In retaliation he wrote to the Dalai Lama and other high Tibetan officials at Lhasa, urging them to prohibit the import of foreign goods, and to avoid having any connection with the English or the Moghuls in India. He asked the Tibetans to keep the latter out of their realms, just as he was planning to exclude them from Nepal.[85] Shortly after this, the reigning Panchen Lama[86] sent two missions to Bodh Gaya in Northern India, sacred as the place of the Buddha's Enlightenment (in 1771-72 and 1773-74), and during the course of these his envoy, Lobzang Tsering, opened friendly relations with Chait Singh, the ruler of Benares, encouraging the latter to send envoys to Tashilhunpo in return.[87] But as Chait Singh was a Hindu and not a Moghul, and was still independent of Hastings and the East India Company, this was not a case of flouting the request of the Gurkha Rajah, and it had no effect on the English.

Lastly, Bengal itself was shut off from Tibet in 1772, when troubles in Cooch Behar to the north, and a subsequent border war between the Company and Bhutan, blocked any chance of trade with Tashilhunpo and Lhasa by way of the eastern passes.[88]

[85] See Lévi, *ibid.*, II, p. 276, and Markham, *Narratives*, p. 158, which tells how the Panchen Lama discussed this matter with George Bogle.

[86] See Chapter II, note 3.

[87] This diplomatic connection between Benares and Tashilhunpo in the years 1771-1774 has only recently been revealed by the translation of passages from the "biography" of the sixth Panchen Lama; although the fact that George Bogle found an emissary from Chait Singh in Tashilhunpo, when he went there, could have implied some previous arrangements. See L. Petech, "The Missions of Bogle and Turner according to the Tibetan Texts," *T'oung Pao*, XXXIX (1949), 335-38.

[88] See Captain Samuel Turner, *An Account of an Embassy to the Court of the Teshoo Lama in Tibet*, 2nd ed. (London, 1806), Introduction, p. viiff.; Sir Ashley Eden, "Report on the State of Bootan," pp. 1-3, in *Political Missions to Bootan* (Calcutta, 1865); and C. U. Aitchison, *A Collection of Treaties, Engagements, and Sanads Relating to India and the Neighboring Countries* (Calcutta, 1929), II, 189-90, and XIV, 72. See also Appendix A, below.

It was not until the opportunities for commerce with the northern countries were tending toward their lowest ebb that the East India Company began to take an interest in the possibilities of trade with Tibet. Probably it was the expedition into Nepal under Captain Kinloch, when the English first had a close view of the Himalayas, that aroused this interest in what might lie beyond the mountains. At any rate, in March of the following year (1768), the Court of Directors in London recommended the obtaining of intelligence regarding whether or not cloth or other European commodities could find a market in Tibet

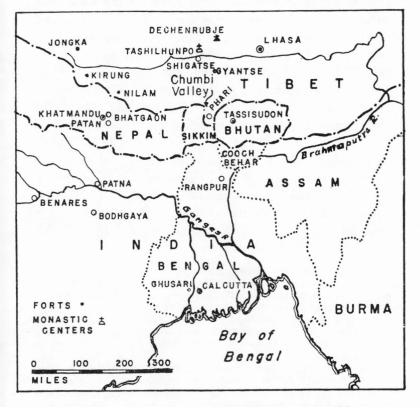

Places involved in Early British Efforts to Open Tibet

and West China by way of Nepal.[89] Possibly it was this that caused Logan to suggest maintaining relations with the old Rajah of Khatmandu as a basis for making contact with the Dalai Lama, in order to further trade with Tibet. Note that the foregoing incidents occurred when Harry Verelst was Governor of Bengal,[90] although his successor, Warren Hastings, is usually given the entire credit for conceiving and initiating the idea of trade between Bengal and Tibet.[91]

Again in 1771 the Directors inquired about the possibility of sending explorers to go to Bhutan and Assam, both of which regions bordered Tibet on the south.[92] A pressing reason for extending the trade of Bengal, and developing new forms of commerce had in the meantime been provided by the great famine of 1770 in that province. This caused enormous financial losses, especially in the export of grain and in the cotton industry, on which the economy of Bengal so much depended.[93] No doubt these considerations greatly influenced Hastings in his resolution to invade Bhutan in connection with the Cooch Behar affair, apart from his other motives of more immediate gains.[94] In any case, the expedition into Bhutan in 1773 marked the first recorded relations of any kind between the Company and a dependency of Tibet, and it led indirectly to the first English mission into Tibet, which left Calcutta the following year.

[89] Sarcar, "Intercourse of Bengal," p. 121.

[90] Verelst was Governor of Bengal from 1767 to 1769, immediately preceding Hastings. See his biography in *The Dictionary of National Biography* (hereafter abbreviated as *DNB*), xx, 248-49.

[91] See the account of Hastings' life in *DNB*, ix, 136-47, and Reverend G. A. Gleig, *Memoirs of the Right Hon. Warren Hastings* (London, 1841), as well as the biography by A. M. Davies, previously referred to.

[92] Sarcar, *loc. cit.*

[93] See Gaur Das Bysack, "Notes on a Buddhist monastery at Bhot Bagan (Howrah)," *JASB,* lix (1891), 59, text, and note 1; and Markham, *Narratives*, pp. cxxxviii-ix. The latter reference contains extracts from the letters of George Bogle to his father.

[94] See Appendix A below.

CHAPTER II

THE FIRST ENGLISH MISSION
TO TIBET, 1774-1775

THE expedition into Bhutan in 1773 proved to be the most difficult type of campaign. Inevitably it resulted in the ultimate defeat of the hillmen, who were relatively undisciplined and had only the most primitive weapons to oppose the English guns. However, it cost a great many lives among the Company's soldiers as well. Just as in the case of Captain Kinloch's expedition into Nepal, malaria and the jungles proved more deadly opponents than the human enemy.[1]

Warren Hastings, as Governor of Bengal, was responsible for the campaign, although the expedition was actually led by a Captain Jones, and this fact was recognized outside Bengal. Accordingly, when the pressure on the Bhutanese became very great, the Rajah of Nepal, who doubtless did not want to see the English become too powerful, called the attention of the Panchen Lama[2] to the

[1] See Turner, pp. 19-21.

[2] This was Lobzang Paldan-yeshes, the Sixth Panchen Lama. See Chapter I, note 61. Hastings, Bogle, and Turner, and other Western writers of the late eighteenth and early nineteenth centuries generally used the term "Teshu" or "Teshoo" Lama, instead of Panchen; while later Occidental writers have used the variant "Tashi." Presumably these expressions were derived from the first part of the name of the Panchen's capital, Tashilhunpo, but in any case they are unsuitable, as they have no basis in Tibetan, and are unknown in Tibet. See Bell, *People of Tibet,* p. 186, note 1. We shall therefore use the correct title, Panchen, throughout, regardless of the term used for him in the sources quoted.

plight of his vassal the Deb Rajah of Bhutan,[3] and persuaded him to mediate with "the ruler of the English."[4]

A letter from the Panchen Lama asking clemency on behalf of the Deb Rajah reached Hastings on March 29th, 1774,[5] and it immediately suggested to him interesting possibilities. He had just been promoted from the position of Governor of Bengal to the much greater one of Governor-general of the Company's Possessions in India, and it occurred to him that he now had a great opportunity for establishing relations between the Company and rulers in Tibet. Especially since one of the latter had technically opened the correspondence.[6] As long as the Company was able to make some very lucrative gains at the expense of Cooch Behar—which was the principal reason why he had

[3] Bhutan, like most of the states under Tibetan influence, had a spiritual as well as a temporal ruler, and theoretically power was divided between them. The Deb Rajah was the temporal sovereign, but at this time the current Deb Rajah had managed to obtain all the authority for himself. For an account of the internal confusion within Bhutan at this period, see Bogle's report in Markham, *Narratives*, pp. 37-41.

[4] The part played by the Gurkha Rajah in suggesting the mediation of the Panchen Lama between the English and the Bhutanese has only recently been revealed by translation of his correspondence as preserved in the Tibetan records. It might be that he merely reinforced a previous decision of the Panchen, who had doubtless already been informed by his Bhutanese vassals of their plight; but it is at least interesting to find that he was active in the matter. See Petech, "The missions of Bogle and Turner," pp. 339-40.

[5] This letter has been reproduced several times in translation. It appears, for example, in Turner, pp. ix-xii, and Markham, *Narratives*, pp. 1-3. See Appendix B below, for another, annotated rendering of it.

[6] Later English writers have emphasized that the special significance of the Panchen's letter was the "fact" that the Tibetans had made the first advance toward establishing Anglo-Tibetan relations. See, for example, Sir Francis Younghusband, *India and Tibet* (London, 1911), p. 5. Those who made such statements overlooked the important point that the invasion by English troops of a state under the suzerainty of Tibet was the first move in this diplomatic game, and that that was an unprovoked aggression scarcely likely to be remembered by the Tibetans with equanimity. G. W. Forrest, an authority on Hastings' administration, gave the equally misleading impression that Hastings, when Governor of Bengal, had initiated a friendly correspondence with the rulers of Tibet and Bhutan. See *The Administration of Warren Hastings 1772-1785* (Calcutta, 1892), p. 302.

undertaken the campaign[7]—Hastings could afford to offer easy terms to the Bhutan Rajah.[8] Then, after having made this gesture of goodwill, he could go on to attempt the establishment of regular communication with the Panchen Lama by way of Bhutan.[9] It is barely possible, although this has never been mentioned, that Hastings had meanwhile learned through agents that the ruler of Benares had been negotiating with the Panchen, and that he therefore assumed that the latter might be well disposed toward considering diplomatic interchanges with other governments in India.

Five weeks later, Hastings informed the Board of the Company that he had written an answer to the Panchen Lama's letter, and that among other things he had proposed a general treaty of amity and commerce between the two states of Bengal and Tibet.[10] At the same time he observed that such a treaty had "ever been a favourite subject with our Honourable masters," and that they had repeatedly recommended the establishment of intercourse with that country.[11]

Apparently Hastings had also developed a personal interest in Tibet. Because, as we shall see, he had obviously read quite widely on the subject, and possessed the map

[7] See Appendix A, below.

[8] See Appendix B, below, for the principal terms of this treaty.

[9] In spite of the actual motives of conciliating the Deb Rajah and the Panchen Lama in the interests of trans-Himalayan trade, the treaty characteristically begins with the statement: "That the Honorable Company, wholly from consideration for the distress in which the Bhootans represented themselves to be reduced, and from the desire of living in peace with their neighbours, will relinquish all the lands which belonged to the Deb Rajah before the commencement of the war with the Rajah of Cooch Behar," etc., *ibid.*

[10] Markham, *Narratives*, pp. 3-4. In this document and elsewhere (*ibid.*, pp. 6, 10, etc.) Hastings speaks of Tibet as "Bhutan," because *Bhot* was the Hindu name for Tibet (*ibid.*, p. 6, note 1). This habit led Graham Sandberg to make the unwarranted charge that Hastings' geographical information was so vague that he confused Bhutan with Tibet. See G. Sandberg, *The Exploration of Tibet* (Calcutta, 1904), p. 102.

[11] Markham, *Narratives*, pp. 3-4.

of that country made by Bourgignon d'Anville. His natural curiosity about unusual places and things, so often commented on by his biographers,[12] must have been piqued by a desire to know more fully what lay beyond the Himalayas.

In the interval between his receipt of the Panchen Lama's letter and the sending of his reply, Warren Hastings took the opportunity to learn more about Tibet from the two men who had come to Calcutta from Tashilhunpo as the Panchen Lama's messengers.[13] One was a native Tibetan, called Padma, while the other was a Hindu pilgrim or *gosain*,[14] named Purangir.[15] These are both described as having been men of acute understanding and ready information,[16] and Hastings learned much from them. He also drew some shrewd conclusions from the presents they had brought him from the Lama.[17] These included gilded Russian leather, stamped with the Czar's double-headed eagle, and Chinese silk, which suggested external commerce; small ingots of gold and silver,[18]

[12] See Davies, p. 429, and *The Oxford History of India*, p. 514.

[13] Turner, pp. xiii–xiv.

[14] Gosain is an Indian vernacular modification of the Sanskrit term *goswami*, and is applied to Hindu religious mendicants in general. See H. H. Wilson, *A Glossary of Judicial and Revenue Terms of British India*, edited by A. C. Ganguli and N. D. Basu (Calcutta, 1940), p. 285. This book explains that Purangir is a fairly common name among these men. Bogle found a considerable number of gosains in Tibet. See Markham, *Narratives*, pp. 124–25.

[15] Purangir was a remarkable person, as some of our later references to him should help to show. Brief accounts of his extraordinary life are given by Gaur Das Bysack, "Notes on a Buddhist Monastery," *JASB*, LIX (1890), 50–99, and S. C. Sarkar, "A Note on Puran Gir Gosain," *Bengal: Past and Present*, XLIII (1932), 83–87. Though he was one of the most remarkable men of his time, he has been so completely forgotten that Graham Sandberg, in his much-quoted book on foreign travelers in Tibet, was able to confuse him with the Panchen Lama who wrote to Hastings (Sandberg, *Exploration of Tibet*, pp. 102, 105).

[16] Turner, p xiii.   [17] *Ibid.*, pp. xiii–xiv.

[18] Turner speaks of "talents of gold and silver," but these metals were used for trade in both Tibet and China in the form of small ingots (*ting*), colloquially called "shoes," and his explanation in the note on p. 345 makes it clear that he is referring to these.

purses[19] of gold dust, and bags of musk, which seemed evidence of internal wealth; and Tibetan woolen cloth,[20] which together with the well-made chests in which the gifts had come, indicated a knowledge of arts and industries.

According to his kinsman, Samuel Turner, who himself later went on a mission to Tashilhunpo, it was after seeing these things that Hastings decided to send an Englishman to Tibet, "on the justifiable plea of paying a proper tribute of respect in return for the advances which had been made by the Lama."[21]

He chose for the task George Bogle,[22] who as secretary of the Select Committee had proved his trustworthiness and capability, giving him the letter to deliver; and appointed Alexander Hamilton, assistant-surgeon to the Company,[23] to go with him. In addition to some valuable presents for

[19] Turner uses the archaic term "bulses" instead of purses.

[20] The Tibetans are famed for their heavy serges, especially one type, which is usually dyed dark red and used for the robes of lamas, known as "truk" (spelled *prug*). The Chinese have long imported it under the name of *p'u-lo*, a phonetic rendering of the Eastern Tibetan pronunciation. See W. W. Rockhill, "Notes on the Ethnology of Tibet," *Smithsonian Annual Report, National Museum*, for 1893, p. 699.

[21] Turner, p. xiv.

[22] George Bogle's biography is found in *DNB* (ii, 764), but a much fuller treatment of his life is given by Clements Markham, *Narratives*, pp. cxxxv-lvii. Bogle never published his accounts of his Tibetan travels as he hoped to, probably because his untimely death interrupted negotiations with a publisher. His papers dropped from sight for a hundred years, until Markham recovered them in Scotland (*ibid.*, pp. v-vi). Graham Sandberg speaks of a large box in the India Office (Calcutta) labeled "Bogle Papers," which he believed had not yet been examined (*Exploration*, p. 103, note 1). However, these are probably the ones used by Markham, who was serving in the Geographical Department of the India Office when he edited and published Bogle's papers, and who speaks of receiving them in a large box (*Narratives*, p. v). Sandberg is very unreliable. Incidentally, Bogle's apparently simple name has been often misspelled. He appears in Koeppen's *Religion des Buddha* (ii, 217) as "George Bowle"; Taraknath Das, *British Expansion in India* (Calcutta, 1929), pp. 2-5, calls him "Bogel"; and the *Cambridge History of India* (v, 45) has "C. Bogle"—this last source says nothing about his trip to Tibet.

[23] Bogle's companion Alexander Hamilton died in 1780 (Markham, *Narratives*, p. lxx, note 1). He should not be confused with the younger

the Lama, Hastings gave Bogle a great variety of articles, chiefly of British manufacture, which he could produce as specimens of the trade in which the Panchen Lama's subjects could be asked to join. Unfortunately we have been unable to find exactly what these were, as it would be interesting to see what Hastings thought might interest the Tibetans. The Tashilhunpo records merely mention that Bogle offered the Lama "presents of glass bottles, etc."[24]

Bogle's formal appointment was dated May 13th, 1774.[25] This announced that the purpose of his mission was to open a mutual and equal trade communication between the peoples of Tibet and Bengal. The means of negotiating it were left up to his judgment. In addition to carrying the samples of trade goods previously mentioned, he was also asked to investigate the manufactures, products, and goods from other countries which could be obtained in Tibet—especially those which were of great value and easy to transport, such as gold, silver, precious stones, musk, rhubarb,[26] and madder.[27] As well as doing all this, he was expected to report back about the nature of the road between the borders of Bengal and the city of Lhasa, the communications between Lhasa and the neighboring countries, and the government, revenue, and customs of those countries. In short, Bogle's mission was to serve as a com-

---

man of the same name who also worked for the East India Company, and later became one of Europe's foremost Sanskrit scholars (brief biography in *DNB*).

[24] See Turner, p. xiv, and Petech, "Missions," p. 341.

[25] Bogle's appointment is quoted in full by Markham, *Narratives*, pp. 6-7.

[26] Rhubarb was considered a valuable drug at that time, and was an important item in the China trade. Presumably Hastings hoped that if it could be obtained through Tibet, it would break the Chinese monopoly in the Canton market.

[27] Dyestuffs were a very important consideration for the East India Company, and madder was especially important in the English trade because it provided the crimson for the Redcoats' uniforms. See William F. Leggett, *Ancient and Medieval Dyes* (Brooklyn, 1944), p. 13.

mercial reconnaissance, concerned almost entirely with trade rather than diplomacy.

The section about investigating neighboring countries may well have been amplified in personal instructions from Hastings, because Samuel Turner, who as a relative of the Governor-general apparently enjoyed his confidence, wrote some years later concerning the preparations for sending Bogle to Tibet:

> The contiguity of Tibet to the Western frontier of China (for though we knew not where they were joined, yet we knew that they did actually join) suggested also a possibility of establishing by degrees an immediate intercourse with that empire, through the intervention of a person so revered as the Lama, and by a route not obviously liable to the same suspicions as those with which the Chinese policy had armed itself against all the consequences of a foreign access by sea.[28]

In addition, Hastings gave Bogle a note of private commissions, containing ten items which are very interesting as revealing his interest in all aspects of Tibetan life, communications, and trade, but especially the latter.[29] For example, he requested Bogle to send back one or more pairs of the goats that produced the fine "shawl wool" from which the famous Cashmere shawls were made; one or more yaks, since their bushy tails were highly valued in India,

[28] Turner, p. xiii. See also Gleig, *Memoirs*, I, 411. The idea of opening another channel of trade with China through her back door was apparently not a new one, for as early as 1768, the Court of Directors had recommended the obtaining of intelligence as to whether cloth or other European commodities could find a market in Tibet and West China by way of Nepal;—again a late measure, because the Gurkhas were already closing off Nepal. See Sarcar, "Intercourse of Bengal," p. 121. For a further discussion regarding this aim, see Dr. Rouire, *La rivalité Anglo-Russe au XIXe siècle en Asie* (Paris, 1908), pp. 145-46.

[29] This is quoted by Markham, *Narratives*, pp. 8-9, and by Davies, p. 429.

and fetched good prices;[30] walnuts for seed, or a walnut plant, and any other valuable seeds or plants;[31] as well as "any curiosities, whether natural productions, manufactures, paintings, or whatever else may be acceptable to persons of taste in England."

Hastings' mercantile interest also seems to have included fear of possible rivals, as he requested further that Bogle should inquire about what countries lay between Lhasa and Siberia, and what communication there was between them; and the same with regard to China and to Kashmir. Apparently he also suspected nearer rivalry, or some seepage of trade out of Bengal uncontrolled by the Company, as he asked Bogle to ascertain the value of the Tibetan trade with Bengal by their gold and silver coins, and requested samples of these coins.

From the point of view of our interest in the mission and in the state of Tibet at that time, by far the most important commission required by Hastings was that Bogle should keep a diary in which he should record whatever he saw that was characteristic of the people, the country, the climate and the road, the manners of the people, their customs, buildings, cookery, etc., or anything concerning the country's trade. Bogle complied with this most faithfully, and the narrative of his journey, together with various personal reports to Hastings, gives us invaluable information on the secular life of the Tibetans.[32]

[30] Yaktails were spoken of in the Indian trade as "cowtails," hence Hastings speaks of yaks as "the cattle which bear what are called cowtails"; though actually their tails are entirely different from those of true cows.

[31] Hastings' interest in plants was not exclusively acquisitive, for he also asked Bogle to plant some potatoes at every stopping place in Bhutan, so that a valuable new product might be introduced there. Markham suggests that these potatoes were probably the ancestors of those found in Lhasa in the last century. See *Narratives*, p. 19, text, and note 1; p. cxiv, text, and note 1.

[32] We have already discussed the fate of his diary and the other papers regarding his journey to Tibet in note 22, above. For some well-merited expressions of appreciation for Bogle's reports, see Holdich, *Tibet*, pp. 92, 98.

At the same time, Hastings gave Bogle a memorandum on Tibet, telling what he knew of its history and customs, etc.,[33] concluding it with the remarks: "I have preferred stating what I know of the subject to putting mere interrogatories. By this means I flatter myself it will be better perceived what information I want, and what information is desirable."[34] This short, concise, but very meaty document not only shows Hastings' considerable interest in history, anthropology, and religion, but it is written in a way that reveals extensive erudition as well as familiarity with his subject. C. R. Markham, who edited Bogle's journal, points out that Hastings' memorandum demonstrates that he had carefully studied all the works bearing on Tibet to which he had access, included De Guignes, Du Halde, Bell, and Astley's Voyages.[35] What is more, it shows that he must have been considering the material and digesting it for a considerable period of time. It must have been only the lack of a suitable opportunity that had prevented him from making efforts to establish relations with Tibet long before.

Bogle and Hamilton left Calcutta in the middle of May 1774, with the Panchen Lama's two envoys, and proceeded to Bhutan.[36] Bogle's narrative of his journey plunges almost immediately into a detailed account of everything they did and found. It reveals a remarkable sense of observation and a great ability to evaluate what he saw. Hastings certainly chose wisely when he picked this man to report on conditions in the regions north of Bengal. Most of the material relating to their travels in Bhutan, however, has little bearing on the subject of Anglo-Tibetan relations, and need not concern us here. The exceptions to this

---

[33] Markham, *Narratives*, pp. 9-13.   [34] *Ibid.*, p. 13.

[35] *Ibid.*, p. lxviii. Hastings also provided Bogle with a set of d'Ánville's maps, showing that he must have studied them himself, and appreciated their value.

[36] *Ibid.*, pp. 14ff.

are his references to the delay caused by the Panchen Lama's suspicion-grounded objections to his proceeding into Tibet, as well as some of his side remarks regarding Bhutan and Assam, which show that, along with the interest in humanity in general displayed in his narrative, he also had a keen eye to the commercial and territorial interests of the Company.

Even before Bogle had reached the capital of Bhutan, a messenger arrived with another letter from the Panchen Lama to Warren Hastings, and one from the Lama to Bogle. The latter said that the sender had heard of Bogle's arrival at Cooch Behar on his way to see him, but informed him that as Tibet was subject to the Emperor of China, who had ordered that no Moghul, Indian, Pathan, or Englishman should be admitted to Tibet, and because the great distance from Tashilhunpo to Peking prevented him from writing the Emperor for permission, Bogle should therefore return to Calcutta.[37] This letter is very interesting from several points of view. First, the admission of the Grand Lama that Tibet was now subservient to the orders of the Manchu Emperor of China revealed a fact that was not yet clear to Hastings. Secondly, it is the first official statement that Tibet had become a forbidden land. However, in view of later developments, it would seem that the Panchen Lama, in his anxiety to keep the British out, might have exaggerated the degree of Manchu control in order to impress Bogle. In any case, this is the first instance of the Tibetans playing off the Manchus against the English, a tactic they frequently resorted to when, after the weakening of effective Chinese control in the nineteenth century, the British again attempted to deal with them directly.

By the same messenger, Purangir the Hindu gosain received a letter from the Panchen Lama which gave as the

<hr/>

[37] *Ibid.*, pp. 44-45.

reason for delaying Bogle's journey, the great epidemic of smallpox which had caused him to leave his capital.[38] Bogle noticed the discrepancy in the two objections to his entering Tibet, but he concluded that, though different, they must have been impelled by the same motive, even though he could not yet make out what that motive was.[39]

When the Rajah of Bhutan refused to intercede on his behalf, Bogle put all his reliance on Purangir, who had encouraged the sending of the expedition in the first place, and was therefore honor-bound to help achieve its success. And he hints that he gave Purangir further inducement in the form of a bribe, after which the latter consented to go to the Panchen Lama in person to urge him to receive the Englishmen.[40]

In a report to Hastings during the enforced delay while waiting for word from Tibet, Bogle concluded that the reason for the refusal to permit him to proceed sprang from a suspicion of Europeans, an attitude that he also found was held by the Deb Rajah of Bhutan.[41] Later, as we shall see, he discovered that this was true, although the deeper suspicions had apparently been held at Lhasa rather than in the court of the Panchen.

The grounds for such suspicion are not far to seek. We have referred to the ill-advised expedition to Nepal seven years before, which had accomplished nothing but to arouse the Gurkha Rajah's hostility, causing him to warn the Tibetans against the English and their allies. And the Bhutanese had considered the Company's invasion of their land, with its attendant destruction, an unwarranted interference in the affairs of other nations—which of course it was. In addition, the temper of the English in India at that time must have been quite aggressive, to judge by some of the remarks of the otherwise mild-mannered Bogle in his letters and reports.

[38] *Ibid.*, p. 48.　[39] *Ibid.*　[40] *Ibid.*, p. 46.　[41] *Ibid.*, p. 47.

In one case, he gives some military suggestions for future expeditions against the Bhutanese, if such action should be required.[42] But he goes on to warn that even if an expedition into Bhutan were successful, he could see no great advantage to the Company beyond what it already enjoyed —the possession of Cooch Behar and no aggression from the Bhutanese. He explains that the trade carried on in Bhutan was scarcely an object for the Company; and as for keeping possession of any part of it, if conquered, or forming a settlement there, he considered it impracticable unless done with the consent of the Bhutanese, which he believed could never be obtained.[43]

His remarks that follow are worth quoting directly. For whether or not they actively influenced the English rulers in India, they express the point of view that was held toward the northern states for many years to come. In fact they were the first enunciation of what was to become almost a permanent policy.

Attempting (to take possession of Bhutan) by force will never answer. The difficulties are unsurmountable, at least without a force and expense much greater than the object is worth. This does not arise from the power of the Bhutanese. Two battalions, I think, could reduce their country, but two brigades could not keep communication open, and if that is cut off the conquest could be of no use.

In all the schemes that I have heard of for an expedition to Nepal, this has been overlooked, on a supposition that if conquest was effected, all the rest would follow of course; but that, I am convinced would not be the case, and when the natural strength of the country is considered, this would appear still more forcibly. For these reasons, I am no advocate

[42] *Ibid.*, pp. 56ff.   [43] *Ibid.*, p. 57.

for an expedition into these countries unless the people should commence hostilities, and then it should be done only with a view to reduce them to peace on such terms as should appear honourable and advantageous to the Company; and this would be easily effected by acting vigorously for one season.

The objections I have made against an expedition into Bhutan hold good with respect to Nepal and Lhasa, for this sole reason, that a communication cannot be kept open; and should our troops march into these countries, they must consider all communication with the low country out of the question till they return.[44]

Bogle's recommendations concerning Assam, however, express a diametrically opposite viewpoint. And they too are important for our subject, because this region and its teas played important parts in the later efforts of the British to open Tibet to trade.[45]

Assam itself is an open country of great extent, and by all accounts well cultivated and inhabited; the road into it either by land or the Brahmaputra lies open. . . . As the great objection against entering Nepal, &c., arises from the difficulty of keeping open the communications; so, on the other hand, the easy access to Assam, whether by land or water, invites us to the attempt.[46]

Assam, as I have already observed . . . yields many valuable articles for exportation. Gold is a considerable article of inland trade . . . when the restrictions against exportation are taken off, it must give the balance of trade in our favour. Supposing it should not turn out so great an object as I have represented, still it cannot with reason be doubted that it would

44 *Ibid.*, pp. 57-58.   45 *Ibid.*, pp. 58-60.   46 *Ibid.*, p. 59.

more than reimburse the Company, by the advantageous terms they would be glad to give us in point of
trade, setting all acquisition of territory out of the
question; and I make no doubt but that, a few months
after our entering Assam, the troops might be paid
and provisioned without making any demands on the
Company's treasury.[47]

Such an aggressive attitude on the part of officials of an
expanding empire could not be easily concealed from the
peoples of the surrounding nations. And it would probably
have been difficult to convince the Bhutanese or the Tibetans that a policy directed against others might not
someday be directed against them. Especially since the
former had already enjoyed a somewhat too intimate experience with it.

In spite of this, however, the Panchen Lama was apparently swayed by Purangir's good reports of Bogle. In
mid-September the latter reported to Hastings that the
Panchen had informed the Deb Rajah by letter that he
had written to Lhasa about Bogle, and had obtained the
consent of the Lhasa officials to his continuing on his journey, provided he came with only a few attendants.[48] This
means that the Lama had only had to consult the Regent
and the Ambans, not the Emperor of China himself, thus
showing that Peking actually did not exercise the direct
control that he had pleaded earlier in his letter to Bogle.

Bogle stayed in Bhutan nearly a month longer, detained
by one of the country's recurrent civil wars.[49] Shortly after
leaving for Tibet, he sent Hastings a report about the
trade between Tassisudon, the Deb Rajah's capital, and
Rangpur in Bengal.[50] In the course of this, he remarked
that the trade with Bengal was very beneficial to the
Rajah and his retainers, and that they were jealous of it;

[47] *Ibid.*, p. 60.   [48] *Ibid.*, p. 49.   [49] *Ibid.*, p. 61.
[50] *Ibid.*, pp. 51-53. The Tassisudon of Bogle and Turner appears on
later maps as Tashichu Jong.

and that while it was possible to show them the advantages
their country might receive from an extension of commerce, it was more difficult to make them see how it would
further their own interests.[51] It seems strange that Bogle
should fail to see why the Bhutanese officials would be loth
to encourage any new measures that might interfere with
their monopoly of trade, especially since his company went
to all lengths to prevent interference with its own monopoly.[52] But where trade was concerned, his usual tolerance
and understanding of others' points of view seemed to
weaken appreciably.

Bogle went on to say in this report that he believed that
the Panchen Lama had no such prejudice as the rulers of
Bhutan; that his territories being the very heart of Tibet
ought to benefit by a circulation of trade and the resort of
strangers; and unless his dependence on China should stand
in the way, he, Bogle, hoped for some success with him.[53]
These words written on the eve of his envoy's departure
must have cheered Hastings, giving him some hope that
his policy might bear fruit; but in this respect they were
somewhat over-optimistic.

On October 13th, Bogle and Hamilton finally left Tassisudon, with Padma, the Panchen's servant, a Kashmiri
trader, and a servant of the Deb Rajah.[54] Nine days later
they crossed the frontier, and on November 2nd they reached
Gyantse, the first large town, where they were joined by

[51] *Ibid.*, p. 51.

[52] For example, see the Company's efforts to establish and maintain a
monopoly on borax in the eighteenth century, described in Wm. Foster,
*Letters Received by the East India Company from its Servants in the
East,* v (London, 1901), p. 124.

[53] Markham, *Narratives*, p. 51.

[54] *Ibid.*, pp. 61-62. The references to Padma are somewhat ambiguous.
On p. 62 he is listed among the members of Bogle's party as it left
Tassisudon; but on p. 69, Bogle says, under the date of October 27th,
"Our party was now considerably increased by the accession of Paima
and six others of the Teshu Lama's servants." (Paima is a dialectical
variant of Padma.)

Purangir with some more of the Panchen's attendants.[55]
Finally on November 8th, the party arrived at Dechenrubje,[56] the temporary residence of the Panchen Lama,
who had left his capital at Tashilhunpo to avoid an epidemic of smallpox.[57] All along the way Bogle kept up his
journal, jotting down everything he saw that might be of
the remotest interest to Hastings. This provides invaluable
ethnographical material even today when we know much
more about the people of Tibet and their customs.

From his first audience with the Panchen Lama, Bogle
got on very well with him.[58] After two or three formal visits,
the Lama received him at any time—except on religious
holidays—without any ceremony, and with no one present
except Solpön Chenpo, his cup-bearer.[59] Bogle, who was
greatly impressed by the Lama as a person, speaks of his
candid and generous nature, his sense of humor, and his
great affability to everybody, especially to strangers.[60] No
doubt their mutual liking for each other had a great deal
to do with the comparative success of the mission. Another
circumstance that helped was the fact that the Lama had
learned Hindustani from his mother, who belonged to the
Royal Family of Ladakh, so he and Bogle were able to
talk together without an interpreter.[61] Moreover, soon

[55] *Ibid.*, p. 76. Purangir is referred to here merely as "the Gosain who
was down in Calcutta."

[56] This place does not appear on any of the usual maps of Tibet.
Bogle's spelling, Desheripgay, is apparently one of his often doubtful
approximations. Sandberg (p. 105) calls it "Deshi-ribgyal" and Holdich
(p. 97) calls it "Desherigpag." The original Tibetan name is spelled
bDe-c'en-rab-rgyas.

[57] Markham, *Narratives*, p. 81. See p. 89 for a reference to his being
there in order to avoid catching smallpox.

[58] Bogle's first audience is only briefly mentioned in the Tibetan records.
See Petech, "Missions," p. 341.

[59] *Ibid.*, pp. 83-84. See below Chapter III, note 81, for the meaning of
the title *Solpön Chenpo*.

[60] *Ibid.*, p. 84.

[61] *Ibid.* Since the Lama had a Tibetan accent, and Bogle a Scotch burr,
these conversations did not always go smoothly. Of one occasion Bogle
says, "He (the Lama) made no answer to what I said. Indeed I doubt

after Bogle arrived, the Lama gave him a Tibetan costume, which he admits he welcomed, as it relieved him from many of the importunities of "that troublesome curiosity which the Tibetans possess in a degree inferior to no other people."[62] Aside from the relief from tension that this gave him, there is no question that his willingness to wear their clothes, eat their food, and conform in other ways to the customs of the country, gave him opportunities to see some of the more intimate details of Tibetan life and politics which would have been closed to the more usual type of British envoy, given to standing on ceremony and feeling the obligation to uphold his own native customs.[63]

On the 7th of December, a month after their arrival, the Panchen's court moved back to Tashilhunpo. Bogle and Hamilton rode in the great procession as part of the Lama's immediate retinue, and the former's account of this occasion and the ceremonies following their arrival are very detailed, as he was apparently anxious to report everything that might be of interest to Hastings.[64] Tashilhunpo was a much more imposing place than Dechenrubje and Bogle has much to say about what went on there. In one paragraph, however, he admits that during their stay of several months, he eventually got rather bored at "these tiresome ceremonies" and the "tedious and uniform" life of the Panchen's monastery;[65] and he was probably much happier when he was working on the account of Tibetan history and politics, and the reports of Tibet's trade with

whether he understood it well, for I spoke in a language he had not been used to, and the guttural R, which I inherit from my mother probably increased the difficulty." (*ibid.*, p. 137.)

[62] *Ibid.*, pp. 88-89.

[63] *Ibid.*, p. 88, Bogle says, "I always like to do at Rome as they do at Rome."

[64] *Ibid.*, pp. 90ff. See Turner's eulogy of Bogle's deportment (Turner, p. 339).

[65] *Ibid.*, pp. 103-4.

neighboring countries,[66] subjects more congenial to him. One might assume that all this composition—as well as note-taking for later writing—would have kept him very busy. But he still had time to take lessons in Tibetan, and to write an account of European history and customs to be translated into Tibetan for the Panchen Lama.[67] And meanwhile he exchanged numerous visits with the Lama, with various lesser Tibetan notables, and with merchants and envoys from other countries.

At one of the interviews with the Panchen Lama while he was still at Dechenrubje, the Lama explained why he had at first refused admittance to Bogle. He said that many people had advised him against letting the foreigners enter Tibet. Moreover he had also heard much about the power of the English, that the Company was like a great king, fond of war and conquest, and as he and his people were peaceful and religious by profession, he was afraid to admit any Englishmen to his country.[68] In fact, he showed Bogle a letter from the Regent of the Dalai Lama in Lhasa, which had been the immediate cause of the letter sent to Bogle at Tassisudon.[69] It began by saying that the Regent had heard of two Englishmen having arrived in Bhutan with a great retinue of servants, and went on to say that

[66] *Ibid.*, pp. 119-29, and Sir George W. Forrest, *Selections from the Letters, Despatches, and Other State Papers Preserved in the Foreign Dept. of the Govt. of India* (Calcutta, 1890), I, 251-54. This report will be discussed in detail in the following chapter.

[67] *Ibid.*, pp. 104, 110. On p. 110, note 3, Markham says that a copy of Bogle's account of Europe has been preserved, but he fails to tell where. He says that Bogle described Europe as it was in 1770: the inns and stage-coaches, the highwaymen, the duels, the parliaments of France (*sic*), and other Old World institutions; and he goes on to suggest that doubtless this document was still studied in Tibet, and was the source whence the statesmen of Tibet obtained their ideas of England and Europe in general.

[68] *Ibid.*, pp. 137-38.

[69] *Ibid.*, p. 131. Bogle speaks of the Lhasa Regent as "Gesub Rimpoche," but that is merely an attempt to transliterate his Tibetan title, *rGyal-tsab Rinpoche*.

the English were fond of war, and after insinuating themselves into a country, raised disturbances and made themselves masters of it.[70] Accordingly, since no Englishman
had ever been admitted into Tibet, the Regent advised the
Panchen to find some way of sending these two back where
they came from, either on account of the smallpox epidemic or on any other pretext. The Panchen said, however,
that after the arrival of Purangir with Bogle's letter from
Tassisudon, he had written a reply to the Regent, saying
that he had from the beginning dissuaded the Deb Rajah
of Bhutan from going to War, while the Government at
Lhasa had encouraged him to do so. Then, when the Deb
Rajah had been defeated, and a great part of his country
conquered, he the Panchen had written to the Governor
(Hastings), who had not only stopped the fighting but
restored all the Deb Rajah's country; and as Bogle had
been sent by the Governor, he thought he was bound to
receive him. He concluded by telling the Regent that if
the people at Lhasa persisted in refusing their permission
against his wishes, if any calamity afterwards came upon
the country, they would have themselves to blame for it.[71]

This letter to the Regent procured Bogle's permission
to enter Tibet, but Bogle reported to Hastings that the
Regent wrote the Panchen to prevent him from coming to
Lhasa, and that he repeated this in several letters after his
arrival.[72] Bogle concluded that the Regent was naturally
of a jealous and suspicious nature, and hence considered
him a spy, but that he was also afraid of giving umbrage
to the Chinese, "as jealous and suspicious as himself."[73] In

[70] In Bogle's general report made on his return from Tibet, he wrote,
"The Government at Lhasa considered me as sent to explore their country, which the ambition of the English might afterwards prompt them
to invade, and their superiority in arms render their attempt successful."
(*Ibid.*, p. 203.)

[71] *Ibid.*, pp. 131-32.   [72] *Ibid.*, p. 132.

[73] *Ibid.*, pp. 132, 154-55. Other passages include the Ambans along with
the Regent as being opposed to Bogle's coming to Lhasa. (*Ibid.*, p. 165.)

addition to this hostile attitude of the Regent, Bogle realized that he could not go to Lhasa with any hope of success without presents to the Regent, the Dalai, the four Ministers (Kalons), and perhaps the Ambans, which would be worthy of Hastings' prestige.[74] In his journal, Bogle admits that in this situation he felt obliged to confine his negotiations for extending the trade between Bengal and Tibet entirely to the Panchen Lama.[75] But he wrote reassuringly to Hastings, "Although (the Panchen) Lama is not entrusted with the actual government of the country, yet his authority and influence appear fully equal to accomplish the views which you entertain in regard to the encouragement of trade."[76]

Bogle would seem to have had ample reason for this confidence in the Panchen's ability to overcome the obstacles to trade. The Panchen Lama was apparently very agreeable to Hastings' desire for opening a free communication of trade between the inhabitants of Bengal and Tibet, and he wrote to the Regent at Lhasa about it, as well as to the principal merchants in the country, Kashmiris and native Tibetans.[77]

Many of these came to see Bogle in person, and others sent their representatives. The Tibetans all excused themselves from sending their commercial agents into Bengal on account of the heat and unhealthiness of the Indian lowlands, which had so often proved fatal to the mountain people. However, several of the principal Kashmiri business houses which had been driven from Nepal by the Gurkhas assured Bogle that they would send their agents down to Calcutta as soon as the rains were over, and the Panchen guaranteed to procure them a passage through Bhutan.[78]

When the officials from Lhasa, who represented the

[74] *Ibid.*, pp. 132, 154, 199. [75] *Ibid.*, p. 132. [76] *Ibid.*, p. 197.
[77] *Ibid.*, pp. 133, 143, 198. [78] *Ibid.*, pp. 133, 160-61, 163, 198.

Regent, called on Bogle in this connection,[79] they began by telling him that the English had shown great favor to the Panchen and to them by making peace with the Deb Rajah and restoring his country. To this Bogle replied that the Dalai Lama was known to the English as well as the Panchen, and that the Governor was very anxious to cultivate the friendship and good opinion of the people at Lhasa also. And he proceeded to emphasize the forbearance of the English in dealing with the Bhutanese, in order to demonstrate that they were not aggressive-minded. When these visitors from Lhasa came to the point, and began to discuss trade, like their other compatriots, they explained that they were afraid of the heat, and therefore customarily proceeded only to Phari Jong, near the border, where the Bhutanese subjects of the Deb Rajah brought commodities from Bengal to exchange for Tibetan goods; this was the ancient custom and would be continued. Bogle then recalled to them that in addition to this trade with the Bhutanese as middlemen, there had formerly been a very extensive direct trade between Tibet and Bengal. He pointed out to them that the Governor was anxious to remove the obstacles that had since sprung up to hinder it, and said he trusted that the Regent and the Lhasa Government would cooperate in this. The visitors replied diplomatically that the Regent would do everything in his power, but that he and all the country were subject to the Emperor of China. The reference to the Emperor's ultimate authority exasperated Bogle, causing him to exclaim in his journal, "This is a stumbling block which crosses me in all my paths."[80]

In regard to the important question whether Europeans —specifically Englishmen—should be permitted to trade

[79] *Ibid.*, pp. 147-48, describes this visit in detail, including the conversation that took place; but it is also described, rather contemptuously, on p. 105.

[80] *Ibid.*, p. 148.

and reside in Tibet, Bogle wrote Hastings that it was a point that he wished to have carried, even though it was not specifically mentioned in his instructions, as he realized it would reflect great credit on his mission.[81] But he had to admit that it was impossible to achieve this permission, in view of the attitude of the hill peoples (Nepalese and Bhutanese), and of the administration at Lhasa. For the time being, at least, there seemed no hope of it. Meanwhile, Bogle shrewdly observed that as the returns for the commodities of Bengal were made principally in gold, any extension of this commerce was so much clear gain to Bengal; and the channel through which the trade was carried on—whether by European agents or Asiatic ones—although of consequence to individuals, made little difference to the country. Therefore, he suggested using Asiatics to conduct the trade, in order to avoid any risk of disturbing the friendship and good understanding which he knew that Hastings wished to cultivate with the Northern powers.[82] This was so fully in accord with the interests of Purangir and his fellow gosains, that one wonders whether Purangir, the artful diplomat, helped to influence Bogle in making this suggestion.

Even if Europeans could not enter Tibet, however, Bogle reported that there seemed good prospects for frequent Tibetan contacts with the English in Bengal. For the Panchen Lama repeatedly told him that he was anxious to found a monastery on the banks of the Ganges which could be visited by Tibetan pilgrims,[83] in order to revive the old religious contacts between Bengal and Tibet that had been in abeyance since the twelfth century. Bogle further said that the Panchen proposed to send some of his highest monks (*gelongs*) to India in the cold season to visit the

81 *Ibid.*, p. 133.   82 *Ibid.*, pp. 133-34.
83 *Ibid.*, pp. 134, 138, 146, 164, 165.

Governor-general in Calcutta, after which they would go on pilgrimages to such places as Bodh Gaya.[84]

Again trade considerations were paramount in Bogle's mind, as we can see from his comments on these proposals. He suggested that the founding of a monastery and temple on the banks of the Ganges would probably tend to remove the strong prejudice of the Tibetans against the heat and unhealthiness of Bengal, and would establish intercourse with the northern nations. Furthermore, he wrote that the safe return of the envoys whom the Panchen Lama proposed to send the following winter would serve to inspire their countrymen with confidence. He ends by saying, "the fondness of the Tibetans for everything strange or curious, strengthened by religion, will probably lead many others to undertake so meritorious a journey; and these pilgrimages, like the Hadj at Mecca, may in time open a considerable mart for the commodities of Bengal."[85]

Even more important than the Panchen's promise to send envoys—in view of Hastings' more ambitious plans— was his assurance to Bogle that he had written the Grand Lama at Peking,[86] who had great influence with the Emperor, informing him that the English were now masters of Bengal; that Hastings, their chief, had shown him great favor, and that the English allowed every one to follow his religion unmolested. He closed with the suggestion that the Grand Lama send some people from China to call on

---

[84] *Ibid.*, p. 134.   [85] *Ibid.*, p. 198.

[86] The Grand Lama of Peking was the Changkya Hutukhtu (phonetically rendered as *Chang-chia hu-t'u-k'o-t'u*, in Chinese). Bogle usually refers to him as the "Changay Lama"; but on one occasion (p. 134) he uses the term "Chidzun Tamba," apparently confusing him with the Jebtsun Dampa, the Grand Lama of Urga. This particular Changkya Hutukhtu will be mentioned again. Commonly known as Lalitavajra (the Sanskrit equivalent of his Tibetan name, Rolpahi Dorje), he was the second Lama to bear the title. See Baron A. von Staël-Holstein, "Remarks on an eighteenth century Lamaist document," *Kuo-hsüeh chi-k'an*, I (Peking, 1923), pp. 401-2.

Hastings and to visit the principal temples in Bengal.[87] In reporting this to the Governor-general, Bogle comments that he admittedly encouraged this, thinking it would be of advantage to the Company to open any channel of communication with the Court of China. And although he was not as hopeful as the Lama about the success of his endeavors, however sincere, to obtain leave for Hastings to send an envoy to the Emperor, he added, "I do not altogether despair, by your favour, of one day getting a sight of Peking."[88]

Even though Bogle saw the possibility of establishing relations with China as part of a larger aim—to benefit the Company's China trade, we have seen above that he regarded the suzerainty of China as the chief stumbling block in his efforts to promote increased trade between Tibet and Bengal. On one occasion when the Panchen told him that the Lhasa Regent's fear of the English was not only personal but also sprang from his dread of giving offense to the Chinese (i.e. Manchus), Bogle feigned great surprise.[89] He replied that whenever the Panchen mentioned the name of the Emperor of China, he was astonished, because from the Panchen's letter to Hastings as well as from all accounts, the English considered that the Panchen was chief of the country during the Dalai Lama's minority, and although the Emperor was his paramount sovereign, he himself actually had full power in Tibet.[90] Moreover, Bogle reminded the Panchen that the

[87] *Ibid.*, pp. 134, 146, 199, all of which apparently refer to the same event.

[88] *Ibid.*, p. 134.   [89] *Ibid.*, p. 151.

[90] This was purely diplomatic language. Bogle knew perfectly well that the authorities at Lhasa were the real rulers of Tibet, as is shown by many of his remarks, like that on p. 197, quoted above. Perhaps this passage is what led Sandberg to criticize both Bogle and Hastings for failing to recognize that they were negotiating with the second ruler of the country, rather than the real head of Tibet. As for Hastings himself, the "Memorandum on Tibet" that he gave Bogle before his departure makes it clear that he realized that Lhasa was the seat of power (*ibid.*,

Regent at Lhasa owed his promotion to him and followed his advice; and that Hastings in his proposals concerning trade was promoting the advantage of Tibet as well as of Bengal. But even such diplomatic acting could not do away with the actuality of Manchu suzerainty over Tibet, and the Manchu policy of discouraging trade with the Europeans in every part of their empire except in the controlled port of Canton.

The other great obstacles to the formation of a strong trade between Bengal and Tibet were of course the hostile attitude of the rulers of Bhutan, whom Bogle had unsuccessfully tried to win over on his way up from Bengal, and that of the Gurkhas. The latter people had not only closed their passes into India and into Tibet, and discouraged merchants from residing in their domains, but while Bogle was in Tashilhunpo they were attacking Sikkim,[91] whose Rajah was a vassal of Lhasa,[92] thus closing still another trade route. The Panchen on one occasion seemed to suspect that the English might be having something to do with this invasion, but Bogle reassured him to the contrary.[93] Another time Bogle tried to persuade the Lama into making a treaty with the English by suggesting that he thought nothing would be more likely to make the Gurkha Rajah

---

p. 10). It seems doubtful that Sandberg could have read this important source book with care, in any event, and like so many of his generalities, this particular criticism is baseless.

[91] *Ibid.*, p. 144. The Panchen Lama did not speak of Sikkim as a country but spoke of "Demo Jong" (Bogle's spelling), its ruler; just as he spoke of the Deb Rajah, or Deb Juhdur when he was referring to Bhutan; and the Emperor of China when he was referring to China. He thought in terms of rulers, not countries, in contrast to Bogle, who had a more "modern" point of view.

[92] The "feudal" system of Tibet caused great complications of administration. For example, the Rajah of Sikkim to the west, was a vassal of Lhasa on the east, while the Rajah of Bhutan to the east, was a vassal of Tashilhunpo on the west; and Shigatse, the great trade center only a few miles from Tashilhunpo and within sight of it, was subject to Lhasa.

[93] Markham, *Narratives*, p. 144.

desist from his invasion of Sikkim than the knowledge of a connection between Tibet and the Government of Bengal.[94] The Panchen refused to rise to the bait, and Bogle never did succeed in obtaining from him any written agreement.

After he finally left Tashilhunpo on the 7th of April 1775—with considerable regret, in spite of what he had said about the dullness of the life there[95]—Bogle stopped off at Tassisudon to attempt once more to negotiate with the Deb Rajah of Bhutan.[96] While he was there, he received a letter from Warren Hastings, in which the latter said how happy he was to learn that Bogle's visit had proved so acceptable to the Panchen Lama, and expressed the hope that it would have the anticipated results.[97] The letter goes on to give a clear statement of Hastings' policy regarding Bhutan and the position he intended it to occupy in the expected Tibetan trade:

The great object of your mission is . . . to open a communication of trade with Tassisudon, and through that place to Lhasa and the most distant parts of Tibet. The advantages of such a plan to the Deb Rajah himself cannot escape him. His capital will become the centre of a commerce the most extensive and the most lucrative, if properly improved, of any inland trade perhaps in the world, and will derive the greatest benefits from it, by being the medium of communication between the countries of Tibet and Bengal. This country is too poor to be an object of conquest, and the expense and difficulty of maintaining the possession of it, if it were subdued, would be an insuperable objection to the attempt. . . . The only obstacle that can oppose your success is the jeal-

94 *Ibid.*, pp. 150-51.   95 *Ibid.*, p. 177.   96 *Ibid.*, pp. 182ff.
97 *Ibid.*, pp. 186-87.

ousy of this Government. This you will find no difficulty in removing, and in convincing him that it is repugnant to every interest of the Company to look to any other connection with his country than that of making it a mart or channel for fair and honourable commerce, which will conduce as much to his interest as ours.[98]

In his reply to this letter from Hastings, Bogle had to admit that in his negotiations he had been unable to obtain the Deb Rajah's consent to allow Englishmen to travel in his country, and that his mission had thus in a measure failed. But he once again emphasized that European agents were not necessarily required for a lucrative trade.[99] His failure to gain permission to have Europeans admitted both at Tashilhunpo and in Bhutan, and his failure to reach Lhasa and establish contact with the supreme authorities of Tibet, both gave Bogle the sense that his mission had not been a particular success.[100] However, he had some feeling of accomplishment, for he told Hastings in his final report, "While the Company's views in a communication with Tibet are only to an extension of commerce, I am inclined to think that the Panchen Lama's influence is sufficient to accomplish them."[101]

[98] *Ibid.*, p. 187.   [99] *Ibid.*, pp. 188-89.

[100] Some modern writers chaim that Bogle's lack of success was at least partially due to the Tibetan rulers' fears of Russia. For these theories and an exposition of their fallacies, see Chapter iv, note 29, below.

[101] Markham, *Narratives*, p. 199.

CHAPTER III

BOGLE'S REPORT ON TIBETAN TRADE;

AND SEQUELS TO HIS MISSION

FROM the Company's point of view, probably the most important results of Bogle's journey to Tibet were his reports on the foreign trade of that country.[1] Their special significance is that they indicate Tibet's far greater importance in the continental trade of Asia in the eighteenth century, before foreign commerce by sea had tended to draw the manufactures of China eastward toward the Pacific, to any great extent; although the wars we have mentioned along the southern borders of Tibet, and the changing economy of Bengal under the influence of the East India Company had begun to cut off Tibet's trade with the countries to the south.

In his first memorandum on the trade of Tibet for Hastings, written at Dechenrubje on the 5th of December 1774,[2] Bogle reported that the foreign trade of Tibet was very considerable. This was because it was a mountainous, barren land with but scant population, and had to get its large supplies from other lands, while it had valuable products to exchange for them.[3] He might have explained too, that the numerous wealthy monasteries were constantly

---

[1] See Chapter II, note 66, above, for references to the first report on trade, and Markham, *Narratives*, pp. 203-6 for a second, somewhat less detailed.

[2] This document was laid before the Council at Fort William on the 24th of February 1775, and copies were sent back to the Court of Directors in London. See Forrest, *Selections*, I, 251.

[3] Markham, *Narratives*, p. 124.

desiring luxury goods; that a large percentage of the population consisted of lama monks, and hence was unproductive; and that the location of Tibet made it a natural thoroughfare—in spite of the difficulties of travel—for the trade in light but valuable goods between China and the lands of Northern India.

Tibet produced gold, he explained, musk, yaktails, wool, and salt, but almost nothing in the way of manufactured goods, except coarse woolen cloth and narrow bolts of serge.[4] The gold of Tibet has been proverbial since the days of Herodotus, who spoke of the great ants in the desert north of India who threw up sandheaps full of gold.[5] Gold is found in the sands of most of the rivers flowing out of Tibet, such as the Indus, the Yellow River, and the Upper Yangtze.[6] In fact the latter, in its higher reaches, is even named "The River of Golden Sands" (*Chin-sha Kiang*).

While gold is found in many places in Tibet proper, especially in the Western province around Thok Jalung,[7] there are religious objections to mining of any kind, lest the spirits of the Earth be disturbed.[8] Sir Charles Bell has explained that the ordinary Tibetan believes that if minerals are taken out of the ground the fertility of the soil will be weakened; while the lamas teach that the minerals were put into the ground by Padma Sambhava, when he

4 *Ibid.*

5 G. Rawlinson, *The History of Herodotus* (New York, 1889), II, 407-10. A Dr. Wilson, in the last century, reported that the gold collected in the plains of Ladakh (Little Tibet) is still called "ant gold" from a belief that colonies of ants, by clearing away the sand or soil, leave the ore exposed (see *ibid.*, p. 408, note 7, last paragraph).

6 H. J. Fleure, "Tibet," *Encyclopedia Britannica* (14th ed.), XXII, p. 177, states, "A remarkable feature is the almost universal distribution of gold throughout Tibet. . . . Every river which rises in Tibet washes down sands impregnated with gold," etc.

7 See *The Times* (London), Wed., Feb. 17, 1869, p. 4, and Wed., Feb. 24, 1870, p. 4.

8 For a rather amusing instance of this prejudice, read about the fate of Tibet's first native mining engineer in F. S. Chapman, *Lhasa, the Holy City* (London, 1938), p. 85.

brought Buddhism from India, and that if they are re-
moved, either rain will cease or hailstorms will come, and
the crops will be destroyed. Bell further explains that the
religious objection is intensified by an economic one. For
when a mine is located, the local people are expected to
work it for the Government without pay, by corvée labor,
so they have every incentive to conceal the existence of
natural wealth, and will sometimes even turn out to attack
those who try to exploit a mine.[9]

In spite of this attitude on the part of the Tibetans,
enough gold was produced to give the country the reputation of being an El Dorado, among the Europeans who
came to Asia. A French missionary of the eighteenth century wrote of Tibet, "There are plenty of mines of gold
and silver, but as the inhabitants do not know how to work
the mines, the metals are only found by digging the ground
at hazard; but this does not prevent their being sufficiently
plentiful."[10] Much of this gold came down into India by
way of Nepal before the Gurkha conquest, so that Nepal
itself came to have the reputation of being a land of much
gold.[11] It was only natural that the English would want to
develop a trade with Tibet, in view of its reputation, so
that they might obtain some of this wealth.

It is surprising that Bogle does not refer to borax, or
"tincal," among the products of Tibet. For this had been
imported into India from Tibet for centuries,[12] and had

9 *People of Tibet*, pp. 110-11.

10 Père P. J. d'Orleans, *History of the Two Tartar Conquerors of
China* (London, 1854: Hakluyt Society translation of the Paris edition
of 1668), p. 90.

11 See Colonel William Kirkpatrick, *An Account of the Kingdom of
Nepaul* (London, 1811), preface, p. iii, first note, and pp. 174-75. The
author intimates that Captain Kinloch's expedition to Nepal in 1767 may
have been motivated by a desire for the reputed gold of that country
(*ibid.*, p. 174).

12 Turner mentioned "tincal" as one of the products of Tibet, figuring
in the trade with Nepal and with Bengal, in his report to Hastings after
his Mission to Tashilhunpo (Turner, p. 382).

been a very important item in the Company's trade for over a hundred years before this.[13] In fact, the East India Company's earliest knowledge of Tibet must have come from a report forwarded to London by one of its representatives in India in 1644, which discussed borax and its place of origin.[14]

In regard to imports, Bogle said that iron, fruit, spices, silk, rice and tobacco, were all greatly in demand, and had to be imported.[15] By some oversight, he failed to mention tea among the things in most demand, but in his "Account of Tibet" he said, "All the world drink tea made in the same manner as in Tartary [i.e. made of shavings from tea bricks, with butter and salt]. Among the great people there is a drinking of tea from morning till night."[16] The Chinese were well aware of the Tibetans' dependence on tea, as well as their desire for silk, both obtained in return for "tribute" to China. Later Chinese writers of the eighteenth and nineteenth centuries have openly admitted that in the Ming Dynasty, tea and silk served as economic weapons to keep the Tibetans pacified.[17]

Bogle remarks that the principal trade of Tibet at that time was with China, carried on by Chinese, natives of Kashmir, and the agents of the Panchen Lama (he might have said, of the High Lamas in general),[18] not all of whom were Tibetans.[19] In addition to imports of coarse tea, of which Bogle remarks the consumption was immense, he speaks of rich satins, ceremonial scarfs (*katas*),[20] silk

[13] For a reference to the Company's efforts to establish and maintain a monopoly on borax in the eighteenth century, see Chapter II, note 52.

[14] See Chapter I, note 79.   [15] Markham, *ibid.*, p. 124.

[16] *Ibid.*, pp. 119-20.

[17] See the *Wei-tsang t'u-shih* (1792), *shih-lüeh*, 1.9, and the *Shêng-wu chi*, 5.2b.

[18] Markham, *ibid.*, p. 125.

[19] Purangir, for example, was one of the Lama's agents, as explained in the text, below.

[20] Bogle refers to these scarfs as "Pelong handkerchiefs." Markham thought that "pelong" was Bogle's transcription for the Tibetan word

thread, furs, porcelain cups, glassware, knives and other
cutlery, ingots of silver, and some tobacco. He explains
that these were paid for by gold, pearls, coral, Indian conch
shells ("chanks"), broadcloth, and a small quantity of
cloth from Bengal.[21] He speaks of this trade as passing
through Sining[22] in Kokonor (modern Ch'ing-hai Province), and fails to mention the road from Szechuan via
Tachienlu. Possibly the latter was still considered primarily as a strategic military road, although it later was
an important route for the tea trade. It is true, however,
that most if not all of the Tibetan trade with China, at
that time, was still in the form of "tribute" from the Lama
rulers of Tibet to the Emperors of China and "presents"
sent back in return—a fact which seems to have escaped
Bogle's attention—and that the route followed by the
"tribute missions" passed through Sining.

According to Chinese sources,[23] the "tribute" from the

phi-ling, meaning "foreign," or more specifically "European" (see _Nar-
ratives_, p. 16, note 7, and Chapter VI, note 73, below); and he explained,
incorrectly, that a "pelong handkerchief" was one from India, or from
Europe, imported via India (_ibid._). However, Turner, discussing these
scarfs (p. 233), says that they are of a thin texture, "resembling that
sort of Chinese stuff called pelong," so apparently "pelong" was the
name of a material. Furthermore, Bogle never makes any use of the word
"pelong" in such a way that would indicate that he thought it was the
Tibetan word for "foreign." Lastly, these scarfs came from China (see
Turner, pp. 72-73), and Tibetans would not have used the word _phi-ling_
to refer to products from China. For the use of these scarfs in Tibetan
culture, see Turner, pp. 232-34, and Bell, _People of Tibet_, pp. 248-50.
We are discussing this whole problem in greater detail in a separate
article.

Forrest, who frequently misplaces punctuation, has separated the words
"pelong" and "handkerchiefs" by a comma, making it appear that "pelong" was a separate commodity (p. 252).

[21] Markham, _ibid._, p. 125.

[22] Bogle spells it "Seling," perhaps because in the Szechuan dialect of
West China (most of the Chinese trading in Tibet, and the Chinese in
the garrisons there, were from Szechuan) n's and l's tend to be confused, and the Tibetans might have picked up the wrong pronunciation
themselves.

[23] The following listing of the "tribute" from Tibetan dignitaries is
drawn from the _Ta Ch'ing hui-tien_ (Kuang-hsü ed.), 67.12b-13, and from
the _Ta Ch'ing hui-tien shih-li_ (same ed.), 986.4b-5.

Dalai and Panchen Lamas consisted of *kata* scarfs, bronze Buddhas, holy relics, coral and amber rosaries, Tibetan incense, *truk* cloth,[24] etc. At the same time, the envoys who brought these gifts also presented *katas*, bronze images, Tibetan incense and *truk* cloth, while the various "Living Buddhas" (*Hutukhtus*), the Kalons, and the great nobles of Lhasa, etc., sent "lucky Buddhas," Buddhist scriptures written in letters of gold, silver reliquaries,[25] and the "Eight Treasures" and the "Seven Gems."[26] In return, the two great Lamas received gold-plated silver tea caddies and vases, silver bells, numerous bolts of satin, and more *katas* (the exchange of *katas* with gifts being an important social rite among the Tibetans and Mongols); while their envoys received a number of very handsome presents, such as silver-mounted saddles, fine robes, tiger and leopard skins, satins and other fabrics, etc.[27] In short, as has been pointed out, the institution of the "tribute mission" was essentially a strictly regulated form of trading;[28] in addition to which the envoys could do a certain amount of selling and buying for their patrons and themselves at established frontier markets, set up at such places as Sining. It was there that they sold their famous Lhasa ponies, and bought vast quantities of tea, tobacco, and other supplies to take home.

The trade between Tibet and Russia, according to Bogle, was carried on chiefly by the Kalmuks, Western Mongols who lived in Eastern Turkestan and on the Lower

[24] See Chapter II, note 20, above.

[25] Literally "silver stupas," *yin t'a.*

[26] The "Eight Treasures" and the "Seven Gems" could be sets of altar ornaments depicting two sets of Buddhist ritual symbols called by these names, or the terms could refer to precious substances in general, such as ivory tusks, rhinoceros horns, and precious stones.

[27] For the listing of the return gifts from the Emperor of China to the rulers of Tibet and their envoys, see the *Ta Ch'ing hui-tien,* 67.13-13b, and the *Ta Ch'ing hui-tien shih-li,* 990.3b, and 15b ff.

[28] See reference in Chapter I, note 43.

Volga, and who belonged to the Lama religion.[29] Probably some of it was also engaged in by the Buriat Mongols, who lived much farther east in Siberia and who were also Lama-ists, for Bogle speaks of some of the productions of Siberia entering Tibet by way of Sining in the northeast, which would be the direction most convenient for them.[30] Bogle speaks of the Kalmuks coming annually to Tibet in nu-merous tribes, with their wives and families, on pilgrimages to the Lama's shrines, bringing their camels loaded with furs and other Siberian goods,[31] in order to combine busi-ness with religion and pleasure. He elaborates somewhat to explain that in addition to furs, they brought to Tibet red and black Russian leather hides, yaktails, some camels, "bastard pearls" (probably freshwater pearls from the Sungari) and silver, which they bartered for broadcloth and amber beads, spices, and gold.[32] However, some of their cargo must have consisted of fine textile fabrics, because, in describing the Panchen Lama's chief temple at Tashilhunpo, Bogle remarks, "the ceiling of the gallery is covered with satins of a variety of patterns, some Chi-nese, some Kalmuck, some European brought through Russia and overland."[33] The writer has personally seen in temples of the West China border region, old lama paint-ings from the interior of Tibet which were mounted in rich brocades of Russian origin.

Bogle found that the trade between Tibet and Kashmir was actually not very considerable. The Tibetan imports

[29] Markham, *ibid.*, pp. 125-26. Markham, who is sometimes rather mis-leading in his editorial comments, notes that the term Kalmuk is used here by Bogle as the equivalent for Manchurians (*ibid.*, p. 125, note 1). Of course this is false.

[30] *Ibid.*, p. 125.   [31] *Ibid.*, pp. 125-26.

[32] *Ibid.*, p. 126. Bogle uses the old term "Bulgar hides" to refer to the Russian leather. Yule and Burnell, *Hobson-Jobson* (London, 1903), p. 125, explains that this term, in general use in Asia, derives from the name of the old kingdom of Bolghar, on the Volga.

[33] *Ibid.*, pp. 100-101.

from there consisted chiefly of sugar, dried raisins, and other fruits, while they exported goat's wool and gold.[34] The famous "shawl wool" came from goats in the regions of Western Tibet adjoining Kashmir, and as already mentioned, was valuable for its use in the famous "Cashmere shawls."

Even if the trade with their own land was not very extensive, the Kashmiri merchants were very important in the economy of Tibet. Bogle compared the natives of Kashmir to the Jews in Europe or the Armenians in the Turkish empire, because of their far-flung commercial enterprises throughout the eastern kingdoms of Asia. He said they carried on an extensive traffic between the distant parts of East Asia, and had formed establishments at Lhasa and in all the principal towns in Tibet. Not only did Kashmiris act as middlemen in the China trade with Tibet, but Bogle also speaks of Kashmiri agents stationed on the Coromandel Coast of Southeast India, in Bengal, at Benares, and in Nepal, as well as in their native country. These furnished their compatriots with the commodities of those different regions, which the latter either disposed of in Tibet or forwarded across Tibet to Sining for the China trade.[35]

Another group of merchants which figured rather prominently in Tibetan trade at that time were the gosains, of which Purangir was one. Apparently they occupied a position out of all proportion to their number, which must have been comparatively insignificant. In his report Bogle calls them the "trading pilgrims of India," and he explains that their humble deportment and holy character, heightened by the merit of distant pilgrimages, their accounts of unknown countries and remote regions, and above all their

[34] *Ibid.*, p. 126. Forrest (*Selections*, I, 252), by faulty punctuation, gives the impression that goats and wool were separately imported into Kashmir.

[35] Markham, *ibid.*, p. 124.

professions of high veneration for the Panchen Lama, procured them not only a ready admittance to Tibet, but great favors at Tashilhunpo.[36] He says that many of them, though clad in the garb of poverty, had considerable wealth, since their trade was confined chiefly to articles of great value and small bulk, and it was carried on quietly, often by paths not used by other merchants. In his account of Nepal and its trade, Bogle says that the gosains had formerly possessed very extensive establishments in that country, but had incurred the displeasure of the Gurkhas by assisting the former (Newari) rulers of Nepal against them, and when the Gurkhas took over Nepal they drove out the gosains.[37]

As for the southern nations, Bogle said that spices, timber, and coarse cloth of silk and linen were imported into Tibet from Assam; and that from Bhutan the Tibetans got rice, wrought iron, coarse woolen cloth and some Indian madder, in exchange for tea and other Chinese commodities, rock salt, wool, sheep skins, and nap-cloth.[38] From Nepal they got chiefly iron and rice[39]—and, before the Gurkha conquest, minted coinage.[40]

Bogle stresses the fact that while the trade originating in Bhutan and Nepal was not too important, these two

[36] *Ibid.*, pp. 124-25. As for their pilgrimages, Purangir, in 1778, obtained a passport from Tashilhunpo to make a pilgrimage to Lake Manasarowar in Western Tibet (see Bysack, "Notes on a Buddhist Monastery," p. 87; a facsimile of the original Tibetan document is reproduced in plate II, following its translation on p. 99). Purangir later went to China, as we shall see, but his travels were nothing compared to those of another remarkable gosain described by Turner, who had traveled in Turkey, Persia, Russia, Siberia, Northern Siberia, China, Tibet and Nepal, visiting Basra, Constantinople, Ispahan, Moscow, Peking, and Tashilhunpo, en route. See Turner, pp. 269-71.

[37] *Ibid.*, p. 127.

[38] The Tibetans are noted for a type of wool cloth, rather coarsely woven, which has a high, soft nap on one side. Peabody Museum, Cambridge, Mass., has some examples of this. This is probably what Bogle meant by "nap-cloth."

[39] Markham, *ibid.*, p. 126.

[40] *Ibid.*, pp. 128-29, and note 1 on p. 129. See also Chapter v below.

countries had been the principal channels of communication for a very valuable trade between Bengal and Tibet in the past.[41] In the latter trade, the Tibetans imported from Bengal broadcloth, otter skins, indigo for dyeing, pearls, and beads of coral and amber, conch shells, spices, tobacco, sugar, Malta striped satins, and a few types of white cloth, chiefly coarse, paying for them with gold dust, musk and yaktails.[42] Probably because they live so far from the oceans, the Tibetans customarily think of the sea as the source of wealth, and greatly value its products. They consider coral and pearls as the finest jewels, and rate ornaments of conch shell almost as highly, thus this trade must have been very important to them, and very lucrative for the Bengalis.[43] At the time of Bogle's writing, this trade had greatly dwindled for the political reasons already cited. But the Panchen Lama told Bogle that formerly the merchants used to bring from Bengal coral, pearls, and broadcloth in abundance.[44]

In his final report, Bogle offered Hastings his ideas on the nature of the trade between Bengal and Tibet, which in some measure supplement the information in his earlier report just cited, and suggested measures which would appear most likely to revive and extend it.[45] The most important commodity, he felt, was broadcloth, which the upper class Tibetans liked to use for their robes, and which was also important in their trade with the neighboring tribes of Tartars (i.e. Mongols). He complained, however,

[41] *Ibid.*, pp. 126ff.

[42] *Ibid.*, pp. 128, 142, 197. Yaktails are still an important commodity in Tibet's trade with other nations, a fact which caused considerable, rather impolite, amusement in the American press on the occasion of the visit of the "Tibetan Trade Mission" to this country in the summer of 1948. See the Washington *Evening Star*, July 19, 1948, p. A-5.

[43] The famous headdresses of the Lhasa women feature corals and pearls, see Bell, *People of Tibet*, frontispiece. In former times most of the corals of Tibet, Mongolia, and Central Asia came from Persia. See B. Laufer, *Sino-Iranica* (Chicago, 1919), pp. 524-25.

[44] Markham, *ibid.*, p. 148.   [45] *Ibid.*, pp. 203-4ff.

that not only had the sale of broadcloth greatly decreased
in recent years, but a large part of the broadcloth used in
Tibet was of French manufacture. Here was the element
of commercial rivalry to stimulate the Company to greater
efforts. The article of next importance, he said, was coral
beads, great quantities of which were used in Tibet, and
also sent from there into Tartary (Mongolia); but he reported that the want of supplies and the consequent en-
hancement of the price had affected their sale, as in the
case of broadcloth. Lastly, he suggested that in addition
to the traditional articles of trade between Bengal and
Tibet, there appeared to be room to introduce or extend
the sale of many new ones, due to the fondness of Tibetans
for things from other countries, and their extraordinary
curiosity. This, he thought, promised a good opening for
the sale of cutlery, glassware, and many other European
manufactures.

Much as Hastings would doubtless have liked to follow
up Bogle's recommendations for the revival of trade between Bengal and Tibet in the interests of the Company,
for the time being he was powerless to do so. While Bogle
was away, in October 1774, the Council of four set up by
the Regulating Act of 1773 to assist the Governor-general
"for the better government of India" had convened after
the arrival of three members from England. The three
newcomers, Monson, Clavering, and Francis, had no use
for Hastings, and constituting a majority in the council,
they opposed him in all his endeavors.[46] Their vindictive-
ness extended even to Hastings' friends, and to Bogle as his
trusted employee. Thus, when the latter returned to Calcutta in the summer of 1775, he found himself deprived of
all his appointments and without employment.[47] Hastings

[46] See the biographies in *DNB* of Sir John Clavering (VI, esp. 460), of
Sir Philip Francis (VII, esp. 616-17), and of George Monson (XIII, 641).
[47] See Bogle's life in *DNB* (II, 764), and Markham, *ibid.*, p. cxlvi ff.

proposed him for a high office, but the three opposing
members of the council rejected the proposal.[48] In this
situation, Hastings could do no more for him than make
him one of his assistants.

In a letter to his father, written on the 20th of January
1776, Bogle describes the situation thus:

> As Mr. Hastings has always patronized me, my
> success in this country depends in a great measure
> upon his fate. His colleagues who came out last year
> have taken every means in their power to ruin him.
> However his merit is so great, and he has done so
> much for the Company, and put their affairs in Ben-
> gal in so flourishing a state, that I hope he will be
> supported. Should things turn out otherwise it will be
> a severe stroke upon me. My Tibet journey has turned
> out as well as I could wish, and although my connec-
> tion with the Governor-general renders me not very
> acceptable to the new members, they have given me
> all credit for it. I am at present, however, without any
> office except my employment about Mr. Hastings,
> and have no near prospect of getting any post.[49]

Hastings managed to persuade the recalcitrant members
of the council to express their appreciation of Bogle's
conduct of his mission to the extent of awarding him a sum
of fifteen thousand rupees in addition to his expenses, but
he was unable to procure a regular appointment until the
death of Monson in September 1776 deprived the opposition of its majority and restored Hastings' power. As a
result of this, within two months Bogle had a couple of
fine positions in the Company.[50]

[48] *Ibid.*, p. cxlvii.   [49] *Ibid.*, pp. cxlvii-viii.

[50] He was appointed co-superintendent of an office for arranging a new
settlement of the Company's provinces at the expiration of the existing
leases, and was also made Commissioner of Lawsuits to manage the
Company's law business. See *ibid.*, pp. cxlviii-ix.

In the meantime, Hastings took steps to grant the Panchen Lama's request for land on which to build a temple beside the Ganges.[51] According to the Revenue Board Proceedings of December 4th, 1775, some thirty-three acres of land[52] on the river opposite Calcutta, at Ghusari, were rented to Purangir as the representative of the Panchen Lama.[53] At the same time, Hastings recommended that the Board consider whether the lands might not be granted as a perpetual free-hold to the Panchen Lama, as it might serve as an encouragement to the people of Tibet to come to Bengal, and greatly facilitate the intercourse of trade between the two countries.[54] The matter was referred to the Directors in London, and when they had signified their approval, two decrees, dated June 12th, 1778, were issued to give the land rent-free to Purangir and the Panchen Lama.[55]

According to one account a temple and house were built there under Bogle's direction.[56] The temple was furnished with the images, robes, etc., which the Panchen had shown Bogle at Tashilhunpo.[57] Another writer says, "There were also guest-houses (as the traditions of the place confirm), in which people from Tibet, some of whom were important enough to have been introduced to Hastings, were lodged." This probably refers to a mission sent down to Calcutta by

[51] A note to Bogle's Narrative, presumably in the hand of Alexander Dalrymple who was to have published it, says that the Panchen Lama wrote to Hastings about his desire to have this monastery, after Bogle's return. (See *ibid.*, p. 138, note 1.) If true, his evidence must have been based on documents since lost.

[52] The exact amount of land granted was 100 *bighás* and 8 *kathas*. In Bengal the *bighá* contained 1600 square yards (*Wilson's Glossary*, p. 132), and the *katha*, or *kattha*, was 1/20th of a *bighá* or 80 square yards (*ibid.*, p. 419).

[53] "The Buddhist Monastery at Ghoosery" (anonymous), *Bengal: Past and Present* xxvi (1932), pp. 195-97.

[54] *Ibid.*, p. 197.

[55] Bysack, "Notes on a Buddhist Monastery," pp. 55-58, 72-73, and 98.

[56] Markham, *ibid.*, p. 138, note 1. [57] See *ibid.*, p. 168.

the Panchen Lama in January 1777, to convey his compliments to Hastings and to offer sacrifices at various holy places in India.[58]

In 1779 Hastings decided to do something more definite toward the establishment of trade with Tibet. For several years the revenue raised for the Company in Calcutta had shown little improvement. Hastings had stopped some of the drains on it, but in spite of all efforts the finances continued to ebb. While the court made urgent demands for remittances, the exchequer in Calcutta was so drained that Hastings could not even cash his own salary bills, and had to borrow money for his personal expenses.[59] In these straits, he wrote in a minute of April 19th, 1779, that as the drain of money from Bengal was alarming, it was necessary to supply that money by opening new channels of commerce.[60] He then went on to speak of the trade that could be obtained with Tibet. On the same day he appointed George Bogle to make a second trip to Bhutan and Tibet, for the purpose of cultivating and improving the good understanding subsisting between the chiefs of those countries and the Government of India, and to endeavor to establish a free and lasting intercourse of trade with the kingdom of Tibet, and the other states to the northward of Bengal.[61]

Before Bogle got away, however, news arrived in Calcutta that the Panchen Lama was about to set out for Peking to celebrate the birthday of the Emperor of China,[62] and this naturally caused a change in plans.[63]

[58] Bysack, *ibid.*, p. 73, and Petech, "Missions," pp. 343-44.

[59] *DNB*, biography of Hastings (ix, p. 140).

[60] Home Dept. Original Consultation no. 1, April 19th, 1779, quoted by Sarcar, "Intercourse of Bengal," p. 121.

[61] Markham, *ibid.*, p. cli.

[62] This was the Ch'ien-lung Emperor, who was born in 1711. Since by Chinese reckoning, he was two years old on his first birthday, he was celebrating his seventieth birthday in 1780. He is very frequently called "Emperor Ch'ien Lung" in Western writings, but that was not his name.

A brief mention of the Lama's projected trip, together with a suggestion for means by which he might utilize this in the interests of the East India Company, was found in a memorandum of July 1779, recovered among Bogle's private papers in Scotland.[64] This begins by a reference to the debts owed by Chinese merchants to Englishmen, and the difficulties of collecting these, or conducting other Company business, without any channel of communication or representation to the Court at Peking. Bogle goes on to suggest that he might take advantage of his friendship with the Panchen Lama to get to Peking, or failing that, to find some official station at Canton[65] through whom representations could be made.

Bogle recalled than when he was in Tibet the Lama had promised to try to procure for him passports to go to Peking,[66] and said that while he had not yet succeeded he had sent a man to assure him that he would exert himself to get Bogle at least a passport by way of Canton. In the memorandum, he went on to say that he proposed to write the Lama that he would get ready either to go by land via Mongolia, if the Lama could get him passports, otherwise

His personal name was Hung-li, and his correct title (temple name) should be Kao Tsung. However, as the name of his reign period was Ch'ien-lung (1736-1795), it is both correct and advisable to call him "the Ch'ien-lung Emperor," a title which both identifies him and states his place in time. For details of his life and names, see *Eminent Chinese*, I, 369-73.

[63] Markham, *ibid.*, p. lxx.

[64] *Ibid.*, pp. 207-10. The date of this memorandum given by Markham, in parentheses on p. 207, is July 1778, but it was obviously written in the following year, for it was not until after April 1779 that Bogle heard of the Panchen Lama's proposed trip to Peking.

[65] Canton was still the only port of China open to foreign trade; except for Macao which was leased by the Portuguese, and was essentially a European town. Therefore the only European contact with the Government of China was conducted through Chinese or Manchu officials stationed in Canton. See *Eminent Chinese*, I, 482.

[66] Previously Bogle had said that the Lama had promised to get permission for Englishmen to go to the Emperor of China, not himself personally; see Markham, *ibid.*, pp. 165, 168, 199.

THE SIXTH PANCHEN LAMA, from a Tibetan Painting.
University of Michigan Museum of Anthropology.
Courtesy of Mrs. Kamer Aga-Oglu

to go by sea to Canton, confident that the Lama could send someone from Peking to take him back there while he was still with the Emperor. He further proposed to send a gosain—apparently Purangir[67]—to Tashilhunpo before the Lama set out, along with one of his own servants, so that the two of them could accompany the Lama to China, and come down to meet him at Canton.

He must have carried out his plans, for Purangir left for Tashilhunpo about this time, and finding the Lama already gone, went on to join him en route. He caught up with the party at Kumbum in Kokonor, where they were passing the winter, and was accepted as one of the Lama's retinue.[68] Continuing on in the spring, the Tibetans reached the Summer Palace at Jehol, north of the Great Wall, on August 20th, 1780.[69] We have written, elsewhere, a fairly detailed discussion of their reception there, from Chinese and other sources,[70] so it does not seem necessary to repeat it in any detail. It is sufficient to recall that the Panchen Lama stayed in Jehol until the autumn, when he returned with the Court to Peking, and that he died there from smallpox on November 27th,[71] after a three-day illness.

[67] He does not mention Purangir by name, but merely describes him as "a Gosain who is in great favor with the Lama, and whom he has sent down to Calcutta" (*ibid.*, p. 209).

[68] A letter from one of the high officials at Tashilhunpo to Warren Hastings speaks of Purangir's joining the Panchen Lama at Kumbum (Turner, p. 454).

[69] *Kao-tsung Shun-huang-ti shih-lu*, 1111.4. This source is hereafter abbreviated as *KTSL*.

[70] "The Panchen Lama's Visit to China in 1780: an episode in Anglo-Tibetan relations," *The Far Eastern Quarterly*, IX (1949), 3-19.

[71] Rockhill ("Dalai Lamas," p. 43) gives this date correctly (conforming to *KTSL* 1122.9b-10) as November 27th, 1780, though he made a bad mistake in the date of the arrival at Jehol. However, practically all the other Western writers who refer to this event give the date as November 12th. See, for example, Markham, *ibid.*, p. lxx, and Waddell, *Lamaism*, p. 239. The Draft History of the Ch'ing Dynasty, *Ch'ing-shih kao* (14.9) has December 1st. An Indian writer, discussing Bogle's career, has "corrected" the date to July 4th, 1780, basing his contention on a letter from the Regent at Tashilhunpo to Warren Hastings, which is

The Emperor of China wrote a letter to the Dalai Lama on February 2nd, 1781, informing him of his colleague's death,[72] and this came briefly into the hands of Fr. Amiot of the Jesuit Mission in Peking, who translated it (rather freely) into French,[73] and sent it to Paris, where it was published the following year.[74] This together with Purangir's report of his journey, which was translated into English,[75] formed the chief Western sources for the events of the Lama's visit to Peking for over a hundred years, though both were full of inaccuracies.

The most important parts of Purangir's narrative, from the point of view of our subject, are his accounts of the alleged conversations between the Panchen Lama and the Emperor regarding Warren Hastings and the English. These are alluded to so frequently in British writings concerning efforts to open Tibet that they deserve to be discussed in some detail.

The first episode took place at Jehol, five days after their arrival, which must have been August 25th, 1780.[76] Puran-

completely inaccurate as far as dates are concerned. See D. B. Diskalkar, "Bogle's Embassy to Tibet," *Indian Historical Quarterly*, IX (Calcutta, 1933), 420-23. Incidentally, Diskalkar publishes this letter as "unpublished," though it appears in the second most important source on his subject (Turner, pp. 449-53). Two of the other "unpublished" documents in his article have been reproduced elsewhere, notably Bogle's famous memorandum on the trade of Tibet (Diskalkar, pp. 425-29).

72 *KTSL*, 1122.9-10b.

73 The Chinese official who had the duty of translating the letter into the Mongol language before transmission confided it to Fr. Amiot, who translated it, taking considerable liberties with the text, and adding unwarranted interpolations.

74 *Mémoires concernant l'histoire, les sciences, les arts, les moeurs, les usages des chinois par les missionaires de Pé-kin* (Paris, 1783), IX, 446, 454. Not long after, it was translated into English, and published by Alexander Dalrymple, the geographer to the East India Co., in his *Oriental Repository* (London, 1796 [as a periodical], 1808 [as a book]), 1808 ed., pp. 273-82. The letter was again reproduced by Turner (pp. 443-48) since it was apparently considered as one of the great curiosities of the period.

75 First published in the *Oriental Repository* (1808 ed., pp. 145-64), this also was republished by Turner, pp. 457-73.

76 Turner, pp. 463-64.

gir describes how the Panchen Lama went to visit the
Emperor and was treated to a special entertainment of
singing and dancing. After this, according to him, the
Changkya Hutukhtu, Grand Lama of Peking, told the Emperor that the Panchen Lama had something special to
say to him "which friendship required him not to neglect."
Then, when the Emperor asked him to speak freely, the
Panchen Lama is said to have replied that in the country
of Hindustan, which lay on the borders of his country,
there lived a great prince, or ruler, for whom he had the
greatest friendship, and that he wished that the Emperor
should know him and think highly of him also. If the
Emperor would write him a letter of friendship and receive
his in return, the Lama said, it would give him great
pleasure.

The Emperor, says Purangir, replied that the request
was a very small one indeed, but that this, or anything else
he desired would be readily complied with, and went on to
ask him about the ruler and his country. At this point, the
Lama called in Purangir[77]—who having been elsewhere,
probably could not have heard the conversation he repeats
in such detail[78]—and asked him to answer the Emperor's
questions. Purangir reports that he then told him that the
Governor of Hindustan was called Mr. Hastings, that the
extent of the country he governed was not nearly equal
to that of China, but superior to any other, and that its

[77] He himself, or the translator, refers to Purangir as "the writer of
this narrative" (Turner, p. 464), indicating that it was a written report;
although the subtitle speaks of "the verbal report of Poorungheer Gosein,"
which might be misinterpreted to mean that it had been an oral one.

[78] Purangir had a gift for circumstantial story-telling. Thus he described in detail the progress of the Panchen Lama's tour from Tashilhunpo to Kumbum as though he had been an eye-witness, when we know
that he did not join the party until it reached Kumbum. By the same
token, these conversations are very likely exaggerated in their content—
if they are true at all—just as the place he gave to them in his report
has given them an unwarranted prominence.

troops numbered more than three hundred thousand horse-men.

The second episode is supposed to have taken place after the Tibetan visitors had moved on to Peking.[79] According to Purangir, at one of the many entertainments given in honor of the Panchen Lama, the latter reminded the Emperor that he had some time previously mentioned to him a Prince, or Governor, of Hindustan called Mr. Hastings, who was his friend, and repeated his wish that the Emperor should know him and have friendly relations with him, by opening a correspondence with him. The Lama went on to say much more on the same subject, to all of which the Emperor is said to have replied that he could assure him that it would give him great pleasure to know and correspond with the Governor of Hindustan, his friend. He also is supposed to have said that if the Lama wished, he would have a letter written immediately to the Governor, in such words as the Lama would dictate; or, if he thought it would be more effective toward establishing the friendship he wished, the letter would be ready when the Lama left China, and he could take it with him and forward it himself. According to Purangir, the Lama decided to take a letter with him, and expressed much satisfaction.

The only testimony regarding these alleged conversations between the Lama and the Emperor regarding Hastings comes from these words of Purangir, the rest of whose report is full of false or distorted statements and much hyperbole, and from the letters—and conversations with Turner—of two high officials of Tashilhunpo,[80]

[79] Turner, pp. 468-69.

[80] It is true that the Chinese official records of the Panchen's visit are too brief to mention such details as conversations, yet if the Lama had actually made these strongly pro-English remarks, one would expect to find them remembered and referred to in the later Chinese documents protesting against the activities of the English on the Tibetan frontiers. But the writer has been unable to find any such allusions.

Chungpa Hutukhtu and Solpön Chenpo.[81] The first of these two Tibetans was the Panchen Lama's brother, and Regent of Tashilhunpo after his death,[82] while the second was his cupbearer and favorite.[83] These two, along with the Panchen Lama, had received expensive gifts from Hastings,[84] delivered by Purangir, before going to China, and they very likely construed—what was possibly true—that the gifts had been intended to reward the Lama and themselves, his two greatest officials, in advance, for stating the English case to the Emperor of China. In which event they probably felt it polite if not necessary, and to their interests, to assure Hastings that what he had wished had been done. Meanwhile, Purangir had all along been primarily an agent of the Panchen Lama and his Tashilhunpo

[81] These two officials appear in Bogle's writings as "Chanzo Cusho" and "Sopon Chumbo." In the first name, "Cusho" stands for the honorary Tibetan title *Kushog*, as Markham first pointed out (*Narratives* p. 91, note 1), while "Chanzo" apparently comes from the Tibetan word meaning Treasurer (*phyag-mdsod*), thus forming the title "Honorable Treasurer." The Chinese records usually refer to him as Chungpa Hutukhtu (or Chung-k'o-pa), and for convenience we shall call him by this name throughout. It presumably derives from the Tibetan *Drungpa*, meaning Secretary or Aide-de-camp, the position which he occupied on the Panchen Lama's visit to China. Professor Petech writes that in the Tibetan records this Regent is called rDa-tsag Biliqtu.

As for the second figure, *Söpön* or *Solpön* is the title of a Chief Steward who also serves as treasurer, and as Turner says of him (p. 248) that all the wealth of the Panchen Lama was entrusted to his care, it is obviously an appropriate title here. *Chen-po* in Tibetan is simply an honorific, meaning "great" or "chief," used to give added weight to the title. Turner, who seems to have been especially fond of long vowel sounds, calls him "Soolpoon Choomboo" throughout his book.

Their letters to Hastings are given by Turner, pp. 449-53, 454-56.

[82] The Ch'ien-lung Emperor's letter to the Dalai Lama (reference in note 72) proclaimed that the Panchen's "elder brother" was to be Nomun Khan, or Regent of Tashilhunpo. (For the meaning of *Nomun Khan* see Chapter IV, note 45.) The title of Hutukhtu given him in this letter and in other Chinese references indicates that he must have been a "Living Buddha," and therefore already a high dignitary in the Lama Church. For a brief description of him, see Turner, pp. 241-42.

[83] Some account of him, and his duties, can be found in Turner, pp. 245-48.

[84] *Ibid.*, pp. 451-52, 454.

faction, rather than for Hastings. He had first come to
Calcutta as an envoy of the Panchen Lama, and if he
worked for Hastings later, there is reason to believe that
he still continued to serve another master at Tashilhunpo.
Indeed, in 1778, not many months before Purangir set out
for China, a passport was issued to him at Tashilhunpo,
describing him as "one of the servants of this monastery."[85]
In short, as a member of the Tashilhunpo group, he might
have been expected to say what the leaders of that group
wished him to.

On the other hand, it is possible that some such conversations actually may have taken place, especially if the
Panchen Lama had previously written to the Changkya
Hutukhtu about Hastings, as he told Bogle he had. For,
although the Lama well knew the Emperor of China's
sentiments regarding foreigners entering Tibet, and was
apparently by nature a rather timid man who might hesi-
tate to provoke his host and suzerain,[86] he was also anxious
to promote trade with Bengal, both to help his subjects and
because of personal ambition,[87] since he personally enjoyed
a monopoly on all the trade of Western Tibet.[88] However,
if they did take place, it is extremely doubtful that these
conversations had as prominent a place in the events of
the Panchen Lama's visit to Peking as the space devoted
to them in Purangir's report might tend to imply.

As the Tashilhunpo lamas seem to have anticipated,

[85] See reference in note 36, above.

[86] Bogle, in describing the Lama's fear of horses, gave the impression
that he was by nature a timid man (Markham, *ibid.*, p. 90).

[87] Turner, in a report to Hastings, wrote that the Panchen Lama was
a man "who was urged to extend his connections as well by an attention
to the interests of those over whom he ruled, as by the impulse of ambition" (Turner, p. 368).

[88] In the same report to Hastings, Turner wrote that in Tibet and
Bhutan the first member of the state was the chief merchant, and that
therefore emulation was suppressed and trade monopolized by the sovereign, and by a few other persons in the highest offices of the Government
whose business was limited to clothing and provisions (Turner, p. 369).

however, their testimony regarding efforts of the Panchen
Lama to establish relations between Hastings and the
Emperor of China made a great impression on the English.
In fact we find the subject frequently alluded to by
European writers in the years that followed, as evidence of
the good relations that might have been established between
the English and the Tibetans, had the Lama not died when
he did.[89]

Almost inevitably, the inopportune death of the Lama
who had been friendly to the English inspired the growth
of a dark legend to the effect that the Lama had died under
very suspicious circumstances. It was intimated that he
had doubtless been disposed of by the Emperor of China,
on the assumption that the latter must have been upset
over the fact that the Ruler of Further Tibet had permitted Englishmen to enter his country, and was apparently planning to have further dealings or commercial
relations with them.

What seems to have been the first expression of this
attitude appears in a report dated September 4th, 1792,
which was recently discovered among the records of the
Government of India. Written by Abdul Kadir Khan, an
emissary of the Company in Nepal, it attempted to explain
why Shamarpa, the other brother of the late Panchen
Lama, had fled from Tibet on hearing of his death (see
Chapter v).[90] This said that the Emperor of China had
learned that the Panchen Lama had established a correspondence with the English Government, and had sent an

[89] See, for example, Gleig i, 416-17.
[90] Published by D. B. Diskalkar, "Tibetan-Nepalese War 1788-1793,"
Journal of the Bihar and Orissa Research Society, xix (1933), no. 12,
p. 380ff. This article consists of letters and other documents, which are
claimed to be published for the first time (on p. 357), although several
had previously appeared (notably nos. 2, 5, 8, 13, 15). This report from
Nepal had been given in Colonel Kirkpatrick's *Account of the Kingdom
of Nepaul* (London, 1811), Appendix ii a, but in slightly abridged form,
omitting the introductory section which told the alleged events of the
Lama's visit to Peking and the resulting rumors.

emissary to Calcutta after which an Englishman had gone
to Lhasa. Whereupon the Emperor had become suspicious
of the Lama and had decided to put him to death, to which
end he had summoned him for an interview. Then on the
night of the day that the interview took place, the Lama
died. "Many said that the Lama's servant, at the instiga-
tion of the Emperor, put poison into his food, and others
spread different reports."

Not only does this sound very vague, but several statements in this passage are obviously incorrect, such as the
remarks that Bogle had gone to Lhasa, and that the Panchen Lama had died on the night of his first meeting with
the Emperor. The whole report was obviously compounded
of hearsay and rumor. Furthermore, as the Governor-general had already received from the late Panchen's other
brother and his steward, who had been with him in Peking,
letters saying that he had died of smallpox there, it does
not seem reasonable that anyone would have put much stock
in this bazaar gossip from Nepal. And yet they apparently
did.

Five years later, Sir George Staunton, in his rather
biased account of Lord Macartney's embassy to China in
1793, remarked that the suddenness of the Lama's death
had excited strong suspicions in Tibet, and said that it
was imagined that the Panchen's correspondence and connections with the English Government of Bengal had offended the Emperor, who "yielding to the suggestions of
a policy practiced sometimes in the East," had lured the
Lama to his Court with intentions that were different from
those which he had expressed in his invitation.[91]

Although Staunton provided no evidence for his "strong
suspicions," we now know that he had undoubtedly seen

[91] Sir George Staunton, Bart., *An Authentic Account of an Embassy
from the King of Great Britain to the Emperor of China* (London, 1797),
II, 52.

Abdul Kadir Khan's report. For a copy of this was forwarded to Lord Macartney with a packet of other documents from the East India House in May 1793,[92] and Staunton was not only Macartney's secretary, but drew freely from the latter's papers in preparing his book. In spite of this shallow basis for his aspersions, they quickly took root, and the legend that the Lama had been poisoned rapidly spread, to persist for a long time.[93]

Lord Macartney, for whom Staunton was writing, was very bitter at the Chinese after the failure of his mission, which we shall have occasion to mention again in Chapter v. Thus it is possible to understand why he might have been willing to disregard the known facts and accept stories of foul play regarding the death of the Panchen Lama. But it is quite easy to point out the fallacies in the latter.

The English must have occupied a very small place in the calculations of the shrewd and powerful Ch'ien-lung Emperor, if he considered them at all in connection with his Inner Asian possessions. He certainly was not sufficiently afraid of them to consider murdering his most important vassal in order to thwart their possible designs on Tibetan trade. In the second place, the Panchen Lama was much more valuable to him alive than dead. Since he was the spiritual leader of the Emperor's Mongol subjects, as well as being both spiritual and temporal ruler among the Tibetans, he could insure their peaceful allegiance to his suzerain.

In fact a desire to cement the allegiance of the Mongols

[92] See Diskalkar, "Tibetan-Nepalese War," pp. 356-57.

[93] The suspicion of an unnatural death was not expressed in the English edition of Turner's book, but was suggested in the French translation by J. H. Castéra (*Ambassade au Thibet et au Boutan* [Paris, 1800], I, 528, note 2; II, 329, note). It was expressed again as a possibility by J. P. Abel-Rémusat (*Nouveaux Mélanges Asiatiques* [Paris, 1829], II, 54), and more forcibly by C. F. Koeppen (*Die Religion des Buddha*, II, 221). It was still cited as a possibility by Diskalkar ("Bogle's Embassy," p. 423) and by Sven Hedin (*Jehol, City of Emperors* [New York, 1933], p. 117).

was understood at the time to have been the real reason why the Emperor had invited the Panchen Lama to Peking, quite apart from the satisfaction he might have anticipated from having a very distinguished guest attend his Imperial Birthday celebrations.[94] It was apparently for this that the Emperor took the trouble to learn the difficult Tibetan language to converse with his guest[95] and authorized the vast expense of building the "Tashilhunpo Temple" at Jehol in which to lodge him,[96] and dispensed the countless lavish gifts for the Lama and his retinue.[97] He would scarcely have been so extravagant of his time and wealth if he were merely expecting to entertain an important but recalcitrant subject whom he was secretly planning to dispose of.

Let us consider once more the reliability of Staunton's remark that suspicions regarding the Panchen Lama's death were being entertained in Tibet. It could be expected that the first news of the sudden death of the great prelate in another country might have excited wild rumors—before the belated return of his entourage in 1782 with the full facts. And naturally such rumors would have disturbed the Panchen's younger brother, Shamarpa Hutukhtu. But we know from other sources that the latter

[94] Fr. Amiot, writing back to France in 1779, announced that the Emperor of China was awaiting the visit of the Panchen Lama, and that he was intending to cement the allegiance of all the Tartars, under the pretence of doing honor to one of the chiefs of their religion (*Mémoires conçernant les chinois*, IX, 6-7). Sven Hedin also emphasizes the importance of the Panchen Lama in the Ch'ien-lung Emperor's schemes to secure the loyalty and subservience of the Mongols to his dynasty, and suggests that the great honors paid to him after his death probably had political motives (*Jehol*, p. 114).

[95] *Shêng wu chi*, 5.15.

[96] *Jo-ho chih*, 80.13-14. This temple was called in Chinese either *Cha-shih-lun-pu Miao* or *Hsü-mi-fu-shou Miao*; the former being a transliteration of the Tibetan name Tashilhunpo, and the latter a direct translation of it.

[97] Some of these gifts were described in Purangir's report; see Turner, p. 458ff.

did not leave Tibet until some time after the Panchen's party had returned, and that his reasons for flight more directly involved differences with his other brother, the Regent of Tashilhunpo, as we shall see in Chapter v.

Moreover the people of Tibet could not have taken the rumors seriously very long, to judge by the Tibetan biography of the sixth Panchen Lama which was translated into English (in abridged form) by Sarat Chandra Das in 1882.[98] This chronicle devotes considerable space to the account of his journey to Peking, giving dates which correspond within a day or two to those in the Chinese records,[99] and even recording conversations between the Lama and his suzerain—none of which, incidentally, mention Warren Hastings or the English in India. This source leaves no room for doubt that the Panchen Lama actually died of smallpox, and it adds the detail that his last words were addressed to Purangir. It closes by saying that the Sixth Panchen was the greatest and noblest, and perhaps the wisest of the sovereign lamas that ever appeared within the snow-girt realm of Tibet; and equally wise and noble was his friend the Emperor of China.

To sum up this long-standing controversy: while the alleged conversations in Peking could have taken place, the only testimony that they might have comes from the rather doubtful words of Purangir and of the two Tashilhunpo officials, all of whom had much to gain from flattering the English. As to the accusations of murder, it is true

[98] Das, "Contribution," *JASB*, LI, 39-41.

[99] If the Tibetan calendar corresponded exactly with the Chinese one in 1779 and 1780, as we assume it did, then all these dates appear to be a day off. There is a strong possibility, however, that the error is due to the translator's miscalculations, since Pelliot warns that all the chronological reductions effected by Sarat Chandra Das are suspect. See P. Pelliot, "Le cycle sexagenaire dans la chronologie Tibetaine," *Journal Asiatique*, 11th Ser., I (Paris, 1913), 649. Unfortunately most of the studies on Tibetan chronology, like this of Pelliot's, discuss the system of recording years at great length, without mentioning the method for months and days.

that while the Panchen Lama unquestionably died of small-pox, it could have been given to him. However, it would seem that the Ch'ien-lung Emperor did not invite the Lama with the intention of disposing of him, and that he had more to lose than to gain from his death. Moreover, if the Emperor merely wanted to prevent relations between the Panchen Lama and the English, there would have been easier and safer ways of handling this than a murder, which, if it had misfired, could easily have alienated most of the Emperor's western subjects in Tibet, Mongolia, and Turkestan, an eventuality he would scarcely have cared to risk.

Whether or not the Panchen Lama ever did urge the Ch'ien-lung Emperor to establish relations with Warren Hastings, and whether or not he was murdered for his pains, his visit to China and subsequent death had an immediate effect on English-Tibetan relations. For the government of Tibet now reverted wholly and completely to the Dalai Lama in Lhasa and his Regent, who were more firmly under Chinese control, and whose party was totally unsympathetic toward English efforts to open Tibet for trade.

Even before the news of the Panchen Lama's death could have reached Calcutta, another blow came to complete the disaster of the second attempt to establish relations with Tibet. This was the death of George Bogle. When the latter's proposed second journey to Tashilhunpo had been thwarted by the departure of the Lama whom he had intended to visit, Bogle had been appointed by Hastings in September 1779 to the post of Collector at Rangpur.[100] This town was the Indian terminus for the caravans from Bhutan, and there he was in a position to encourage the northern trade and to superintend the annual fair, which was attended by Bhutanese and Tibetans. (It has been said

[100] Markham, *ibid.*, p. cli.

that Bogle started this fair in 1780, but it seems more probable that he only gave encouragement to an already existing institution.[101]) While there, he received a letter from Hastings asking him to come down to Calcutta to a better position. But shortly after he reached that city, he contracted cholera, from which he died on April 3rd, 1781, at the early age of thirty-four.[102]

[101] The biography of Bogle in *DNB* (II, 764) says that in 1779 he was appointed collector of Rangpur where he established a fair. Markham (*Narratives*, p. cli) speaks of the annual fair at Rangpur, as though it was already a regular thing; but another reference to it (*ibid.*, p. cliii) is slightly ambiguous, and might have misled the author of the biography in *DNB*. The fair had probably already been an annual thing for years, on the occasion of the coming of the trading caravan from Bhutan. See Appendix c, below, article 4.

[102] Markham, *ibid.*, p. cliv. He was buried in Calcutta, and his tomb may still be seen there in the South Park Street Cemetery. See "The Buddhist Monastery at Ghoosery," p. 195. Incidentally Bogle had a town in Bengal named in his honor, Boglepur, where Robert Saunders (see next chapter) later served as medical officer; the suffix *-pur* is an Indian word meaning "town." See *Philosophical Transactions of the Royal Society of London*, LXXIX (1789), 79.

CHAPTER IV

SAMUEL TURNER'S MISSION TO TIBET

IN 1783

THE sudden deaths of Bogle and the Panchen Lama presented a great setback to Hastings' plan for promoting and extending the Company's trade with the northern countries. However, he held such firm convictions about the advantages to be derived from such a trade that he was not daunted.

On the 12th of February 1782, Purangir returned to Calcutta and reported to Hastings about his long journey to Peking. He brought with him letters from the Regent of Tashilhunpo, Chungpa Hutukhtu, and his steward, Solpön Chenpo. These messages expressed great cordiality and friendship toward Hastings, and gave him hope that the Tibetans at Tashilhunpo were still inclined to cooperate with his plans for trade.[1] Shortly after, word reached Calcutta that the Panchen Lama's reincarnation had been discovered in the person of a child.[2]

The time seemed ripe for another venture toward opening trade contacts with the North as the international

[1] Translations of the letters are given in Turner, pp. 449-53, 454-56. It was probably at the time that he delivered these, that Purangir made his famous report. There was also a note from Solpön Chenpo to Bogle, since the news of the latter's death had not reached Tibet, see Diskalkar, pp. 436-38.

[2] See Turner, p. xvii. Markham (*Narratives*, p. lxxi) says that on February 12th, 1782, the news arrived in Calcutta that the Panchen Lama had reappeared in the person of an infant; but this was not true, according to Turner's account (*loc.cit.*).

situation had greatly improved, affecting the outlook in India. The American Revolution had just recently ended, and the attendant war with France and her allies in India was drawing to a close. As a result, sea commerce was beginning to move freely once more.[3] Hastings had reason to anticipate a renewed flood of manufactured goods from Britain, and it would be necessary to find wider markets for them.

With these favorable prospects, Hastings planned to send another English mission to Tibet in order to discuss the possibilities for trade there. He resolved to do this under the pretext of sending an envoy to congratulate the Regent and present his regards to his old friend the Lama in his new reincarnation.[4] Whatever he thought about the Tibetan concept of reincarnation, he was quite willing to give the appearance of taking it seriously if that would encourage the good will of the Tibetans, and he expected his subordinates to do likewise. (Only by realizing this attitude is it possible to understand some of the naïve-sounding remarks of the latter.)

Having decided to send the mission, Hastings appointed to represent him his kinsman, Samuel Turner, who was a lieutenant in the army of the East India Company.[5] On January 9th, 1783, Turner received his formal nomination.[6] At the same time, Lieutenant Samuel Davis, an accomplished draughtsman, and Dr. Robert Saunders, a

[3] Turner later discussed this international situation with the Regent at Tashilhunpo (p. 276).

[4] Sandberg again makes the false accusation that Hastings supposed the Tashilhunpo Lama to be the genuine monarch of Tibet, and that he made a great mistake in not dispatching his missions to the Dalai Lama at Lhasa. "In that way it was," says he, "that China in the 18th century gained the position of ascendancy which might have been obtained by the Government of India." *Exploration of Tibet*, p. 107.

[5] See Turner's biography in *DNB*, xix, pp. 1281-82, also Markham, *ibid.*, p. lxxi, note 2, and Sandberg, *Exploration*, p. 111, note 1.

[6] Turner, p. xvii.

medical officer, were detailed to be the other members of the party.[7]

Turner, like Bogle before him, was directed to proceed first to Bhutan, to try to make some further arrangements for trade with that country. This seemed especially necessary, as two intervening missions since that of Bogle, under the direction of Alexander Hamilton, in 1776 and 1777, had not accomplished very much beyond maintaining an irregular contact between Hastings and the Rajah of Bhutan,[8] and the situation was rather frustrating to the Company's aspirations for wider trade.

Leaving Calcutta soon after they received their orders,[9] the three Englishmen went first to Rangpur, where they obtained passports from the Deb Rajah to permit them to enter Bhutan.[10] Then they continued along the route that had been taken by Bogle. Turner immediately began to write down a detailed account of the trip, as Bogle had done, for he had apparently received similar instructions from Hastings.[11] Later this formed the basis for his famous book.

As he was temperamentally somewhat different from

[7] See the account of Davis's life in Markham, *ibid.*, p. lxxi, note 3. As he never got beyond Bhutan, he is not very important in the story of the English efforts to open Tibet; but his son, Sir John Davis, as the first British Minister to China, played a part in the abortive efforts to get China to open Tibet to trade in the 1840's. Samuel Davis, an accomplished artist, contributed most of the illustrations in Turner's book.

Robert Saunders, another remarkably observant man, wrote "Some Account of the Vegetable and Mineral Productions of Boutan and Thibet," published in *Philosophical Transactions of the Royal Society of London*, LXXIX (1789), 79-111, and republished in Turner, pp. 387-416.

[8] See Markham, *ibid.*, pp. lxix-lxx.

[9] Turner (p. 3) fails to give the exact date.

[10] Turner, p. 5.

[11] Turner not only kept a journal and wrote a thorough report on trade conditions, but he also arranged to obtain two yaks, which he sent on to Hastings in England, after the latter had left India. One of these survived the voyage, and no doubt became a great curiosity in England (*ibid.*, pp. 188-89). His attempt to bring out some "shawl goats" and later to send them to England, to gratify Hastings' fondness for strange animals, was less successful (*ibid.*, pp. 356-57).

Bogle, Turner in his narrative was perhaps a little less concerned with trade, and more with items of general human interest. Probably it is this characteristic which has caused later writers to speak of Turner's mission as having been something of a leisurely pleasure trip, and to deride his lack of earnestness.[12] But such remarks seem ill-founded. Perhaps Turner did write too enthusiastically about his skating, but Bogle also liked horse-racing.[13] And on the whole, Turner's account compares very favorably with Bogle's in its observations on the life and culture of Bhutan and Tibet. One has only to read Turner's trade report to Hastings, which is summarized below, to see that he too was capable of making penetrating judgments and shrewd recommendations.[14]

When the mission reached the capital of Bhutan, it was detained there for some time by a civil war.[15] As Bogle had had the same difficulty, Turner remarked that rebellion must be a chronic condition in that country. Finally on the 8th of September, Turner and Saunders were able to leave Tassisudon for Tibet.[16] The very talented Davis had to be left behind, as the Tibetans insisted that they could not admit any more Englishmen than they had on the previous occasion.[17] When we see his magnificent sketches of the Bhutanese landscape, illustrating Turner's book, it seems especially regrettable that he was not permitted to enter Tibet and make some more drawings there, for Turner's own sketches of Tibetan scenes leave much to be desired.

On the 22nd of September 1783, the party reached

---

[12] See the derogatory remarks made by Sandberg in *Exploration*, pp. 108, 111. On the former page he says sarcastically, "They were travelling at Government charges and evidently were determined to have an enjoyable outing."

[13] See Turner, pp. 331-32, 355, and Markham, *ibid.*, p. 79, for these young gentlemen's love of sports.

[14] Turner, pp. 361-84.   [15] *Ibid.*, Chapter VI (107ff.) and p. 148.

[16] *Ibid.*, p. 168.   [17] *Ibid.*, pp. 161, 168.

Tashilhunpo,[18] where they were welcomed by the attendants of the Regent and the Solpön Chenpo, and on the following morning they were received by these dignitaries in personal audiences.[19]

On this occasion the Regent assured Turner that the present Panchen Lama was the same person as the preceding one. However, since his spirit had only just returned to the world, he was still merely an infant and incapable of action.[20] Then he went on to recall the old Panchen's visit to Peking, telling how the latter had begun to speak to the Emperor of China about Mr. Hastings, confident of the Emperor's sanction and trusting that the good relations between them would extend its influence over all the Lama's votaries and all the subjects of both empires.[21] This sounds like pure diplomatic flattery, echoing the substance of the Regent's previous letter to Hastings, and like the latter it cannot be considered as definitely proving that such conversations in Peking actually took place.

Returning to the topic of the new Panchen, the Regent told Turner that as soon as the Emperor of China had heard of his regeneration, the latter had sent an embassy with letters of congratulation. In these, he had strictly commanded both the Regent and his assistant to be very careful of the young Lama, to have him educated in the strictest privacy, and to prevent any strangers from coming into his presence.[22] This last injunction sounds as though it had been deliberately aimed at the English, for the Lama's Mongol and Tibetan believers would not have been considered as "strangers."

18 Turner does not give the date precisely, but on p. 226, he speaks of leaving Gyantse on September 20th, and he arrived at Tashilhunpo two days later.

19 Turner, pp. 232ff. For the Solpön Chenpo's status at this time, which amounted practically to Vice-Regent, see *ibid.*, p. 246. Turner says that he was treated by the Regent as a colleague rather than as a subordinate, and his opinion was awaited on every occasion.

20 *Ibid.*, pp. 238-39.   21 *Ibid.*, p. 239.   22 *Ibid.*

In his interview with Solpön Chenpo, the latter told
Turner of the difficulty he and the Regent had had in
contriving to get the Englishmen to Tashilhunpo.[23] Turner comments on the Tibetans' recital of the troubles they
had faced in trying to get him in, saying that even though
they were averse to admitting any direct dependence on
China, he could plainly detect that they had the greatest
awe of the Emperor, of his Residents and officials, and of
the Lhasa Regent, who had usurped most of the Dalai
Lama's temporal power.[24] He realized, as had Bogle, that
the power of the Chinese—or rather, the Manchus—and
of the Regent at Lhasa were insurmountable barriers to
any permanent negotiations at that time.

On a later occasion, when Turner brought up the matter
of trade with Bengal, the Regent told him that many
letters on the subject had passed between him and the Dalai
Lama, who was always favorably inclined toward the English. Chungpa principally blamed the Regent at Lhasa for
the discouragements and obstructions to better relations,
but he also referred with emphasis to the Chinese.[25] This
harking back to the Chinese caused Turner to observe that
the influence of the Chinese Court seemed to overawe the
Tibetans in all their dealings, and produced a caution and
timidity in their conduct. But he also noticed that they
disliked the interference of the Chinese. He found that
when the Chinese (or Manchu) officials came to Tashilhunpo, they were treated with the utmost reserve, even
when they had come only to reverence the Panchen Lama.
The Tibetans did not permit the Chinese envoys to stay
inside the limits of the monastery, and were openly impatient during their visit, assuming an unusual air of

23 *Ibid.*, p. 244.
24 *Ibid.*, p. 245. This was not the same Regent of Lhasa who had
plagued Bogle, though Turner gives him the same name (with slightly
variant spelling). See note 45, below.
25 *Ibid.*, p. 253.

secrecy to prevent their finding out anything about local affairs. Then when the Chinese were ready to leave, the Tibetans announced their departure with much apparent satisfaction.[26]

In regard to his discussion with the Regent and Solpön Chenpo about Tibetan views of the outside world, Turner mentions their attitude toward Russia. (This seems especially interesting in view of the later Anglo-Russian rivalry over Tibet that culminated in the Younghusband Expedition to Lhasa in 1904.) He found that the Tibetans knew about the reigning Czarina, Catherine the Great, as well as the extent of her dominions and the commerce that was carried on between Russia and China. He also learned that Russia had made many overtures in an effort to extend her trade to the inner parts of Tibet. But the disinclination of the Tibetans to make any foreign connections, and the watchful jealousy of the Chinese, had defeated every such attempt.[27]

The Lamas told him further that some years before, Catherine had invited the Jebtsun Dampa Hutukhtu, Grand Lama of Urga, to correspond with her, and had sent ambassadors to his palace in Mongolia to bring him a number of presents. The Grand Lama had forwarded the letter and presents to Tashilhunpo to ask the Panchen's advice. (Turner was shown an illustrated Russian Bible which had been one of these gifts.) The Panchen Lama had given the Russians little encouragement, although he did consent to let them have a limited intercourse with Urga.[28] It is important to note, however, that there is no

[26] *Ibid.*, pp. 253-54.   [27] *Ibid.*, pp. 272-73.

[28] *Ibid.*, p. 273. Turner speaks of the Grand Lama of Urga as "Taranaut Lama," since his religious name was Taranatha; and he speaks of his place of residence as "Karka," which apparently stands for "Khalkha," the tribal name of the Outer Mongolians whose territory included Urga.

evidence that he ever had any apprehensions about possible Russian designs on Tibet, as later writers have alleged.[29]

In discussing commerce in general, the Regent expressed particular admiration at the bold spirit of enterprise that animated the British nation. But Turner was rather distressed to find that he attributed the motive that impelled so many Englishmen to leave their friends and their country, braving the dangers of bad climates and unfriendly men, to some grave internal defect of their own land.[30]

When winter drew near, and it became time for the Englishmen to leave, the Regent granted Turner a last audience on the 30th of November. At this time he presented him with gifts and letters for Hastings, and asked Turner to remember his unchanged and steady friendship. He assured him that even though the Tashilhunpo Lamas were then helpless to do anything because of the infancy of the Panchen Lama, when the latter came of age and resumed his throne, all would be well.[31]

[29] A Chinese political scientist, W. K. Lee, has written that one reason for Bogle's failure to conclude the treaty he desired with the Panchen Lama was the deference of the Lhasa Government to Russia's possible displeasure; and that Turner also failed in a similar aim, because the Tibetan regent was still afraid of Russian as well as Chinese influences. See Wei Kuo Lee, *Tibet in Modern World Politics, 1744-1922* (New York, 1931), p. 16.

An Indian writer, Taraknath Das, even more specifically states that "according to the report of Bogel [*sic*], as early as that time (1774-1775), the Tashi Lama had certain ideas about the importance of Russian and Russo-Chinese relations affecting Tibet"; and he lists as the third of three distinct obstacles in the way of establishing Anglo-Tibetan relations in the 18th century, "growing Russian interest toward Tibet." See Taraknath Das, *British Expansion in Tibet* (Calcutta, 1929), p. 4. These statements represent a reading of later trends back into an earlier period, and they are quite unsubstantiated by anything in the reports of Bogle's or Turner. Bogle's formal reports do not mention Russia, and in his journal, he merely remarks that the Panchen Lama had commented that Russia and China were on bad terms, and that he wished to know how he could best bring about peace if war should break out, because that was "the business of us Lamas." The Lama's anxiety to keep the peace apparently had no elements of personal apprehension for his own safety or that of his realms.

[30] Turner, p. 277.   [31] *Ibid.*, pp. 327-28.

On December 2nd Turner and Saunders started home. Two days later they stopped off at Terpaling to visit the infant Panchen and give him Hastings' presents.[32] The Regent had previously refused to permit Turner to see him, probably because of the warning sent by the Emperor, but presumably he consented to this informal meeting as he himself would not be present, and therefore could not be directly implicated.[33] In any case, Turner could never have gained access to the child-Lama without the Regent's consent.

The Tibetan records of the occasion are somewhat fuller than usual. First they describe the gifts: Hastings had sent pearls, fine coral earrings, a jewelled watch, spectacles, two pieces of special Russian cloth, and silver cups containing spices, cloves and nutmegs; while Turner presented some woolen hats, pieces of gold brocade, etc.[34] These made a great impression on the Tibetans; but they were no less impressed by the Englishmen's reverence for the child Lama. Their account says, "Although [the visitors] were not knowers of the niceties of religion, by merely gazing [at the young Panchen] an irrepressible faith was born in them. And they said: 'In such a little frame there are activities of body, speech and mind, so greatly marvelous and different from the others!' Thus they spoke with great reverence."[35] This was not the mere courteous flattery on Turner's part that the Governor-general would have expected of him. He was genuinely impressed by the young incarnation, and said so to Hastings. The latter was so much interested in Turner's description of the interview

[32] *Ibid.*, pp. 329, 332ff.

[33] The previous refusal was on the occasion of the young Lama's installation at Terpaling, when Chinese officials were expected to be present, which suggests that the Regent interpreted the Chinese Emperor's orders to exclude strangers as applying to the English. See *ibid.*, pp. 248-49. For the consent, see pp. 378-79.

[34] See Petech, "Missions," pp. 344-45.   [35] *Ibid.*, p. 335.

that he wrote about it to several friends.[36] And it has been quoted as an item of human interest in a number of books about Tibet that have been written since.

The most significant feature of this interview from the point of view of the objectives of his mission was that Turner had an opportunity to assure the young Panchen that Hastings had been overwhelmed with grief and sorrow on receiving the news of his death in China, and that Hastings was hopeful that the former friendship between them would increase. So that by the Lama's continuing demonstration of kindness to the English, there might be an extensive communication between his people and the British dependents in India.[37]

The effect of Turner's diplomatic speech became apparent to him on the following day. At an interview with the parents of the Lama, the father declared himself favorable to the English cause, and said that he hoped for a lasting friendship.[38] The idea of trade relations with India would naturally appeal to him, because any increase in the commerce between Tashilhunpo and Bengal would enrich him as well as his son. Turner found him a very likable person with a fondness for sports, and after leaving diplomatic subjects, the two of them had a long discussion of archery and rifle shooting, finding much in common.[39] If the Lama's father had had more immediate influence, the mission would have been a great success.

On the 6th of December, Turner called on the Panchen Lama twice more,[40] and on the following day he set out once again for Bengal. On the way, he and Saunders stopped off in Bhutan for a few interviews with the Deb

36 See Gleig, III, 161-62. The original account of the interview is quoted in Forrest, *Selections*, III, 1079-81.

37 Turner, pp. 334-35. No doubt Hastings did actually grieve very much at the old Lama's death, but his reasons for grief were doubtless more material than sentimental, lamenting the inevitable setback to his plans for furthering the northern trade of Bengal.

38 *Ibid.*, pp. 339ff.   39 *Ibid.*, pp. 341ff.   40 *Ibid.*, pp. 344-46.

Rajah, which did not come to much. They left there on December 30th to go on to Rangpur,[41] and in March 1784 Turner joined Hastings at Patna,[42] to report on the results of his trip.[43]

In his written report, Turner remarked that the unfortunate accidents which had prevented Bogle's proposed second journey to Tashilhunpo, and the untimely death of the Panchen Lama himself, were events that seemed likely in themselves to destroy the effects of all the former efforts to open Tibet to trade. For these were enough to revive in the minds of the Tibetans, who were naturally opposed to innovations, all their former distrust of foreigners, thus interrupting the growing confidence that had been built up by previous relations.[44]

He went on to say that as partial compensation for the above-mentioned disasters, the death of the old Regent of Lhasa, who had been violently opposed to all relations with the English and had blocked Bogle's more ambitious efforts, had appeared to offer a new prospect for opening communications. However, his successor, the new Regent,[45] not only shared the same prejudices toward the English, but, since the discussions of the old Lama with the Emperor of China regarding the position of the Dalai Lama had almost cost him his power, he was particularly jealous of

[41] *Ibid.*, pp. 357-58.

[42] Hastings was on his way to Lucknow. See Gleig, III, 161-62.

[43] Turner, p. 358. The report follows as Part III of Turner's book. It is also presented in Forrest, *Selections*, III, 1070-79.

[44] *Ibid.*, p. 364.

[45] Turner's references to the new Regent at Lhasa are rather confusing, as he speaks of both the old one (p. 364) and the new one (pp. 245-53) as "Gesub Rimbochay," which as we have seen (Chapter II, note 69), was the Tibetan title pertaining to the office of Regent. However, he also speaks of the new one as "Raja Nimoheim" (p. 365) which is a rather ludicrous combination of his Indian title of *Rajah*, and his Mongol one of *Nomun Khan*. This is especially redundant since *Nomun Khan* is the Mongol equivalent of the Sanskrit title, *Dharmaraja*, "King of the Law." The Regents, or secular kings, of Tibet—like the co-ruler of Bhutan—bore the official title of *Dharmaraja*.

the Panchen Lama's party and actively hostile to it. He therefore took every opportunity to thwart the designs of Tashilhunpo regarding trade with Bengal.[46]

Turner thought, however, that the Regent at Lhasa would lose his power when the new Panchen Lama came of age and assumed the throne, and that then the Dalai Lama would have unrestricted control over the government of Tibet. Then, when this happened, if the Panchen had been made to resume the plans he had projected in his supposed preexistence, for the recovery of the prerogatives that rightly belonged to the Grand Lamas but had been usurped by their regents, the same consistency of conduct would certainly prompt him to reconsider the negotiations of 1775 and the plans for a free commerce between Tibet and Bengal. This seemed especially likely since the old Panchen's desire for such a trade had apparently been motivated by a selfish interest to extend his privileges of monopolistic trade,[47] and such an extension would also benefit the new Lama.

Turner pointed out, in fact, that there was every probability that the young Panchen would assume office with strong impulses towards encouraging relations with the English.[48] For, since the usual proof of the identity of a reincarnated Lama (aside from auspicious birthmarks, etc.) was his early recognition of the possessions, friends, and transactions of his previous existence, the new Lama would doubtless be deliberately taught to resume the interests and tendencies of the former Panchen Lama, as one of the strongest proofs of his identity, in order to win the acceptance of his people.[49]

Turner reported that the Regent of Tashilhunpo had shown the strongest inclinations toward encouraging and assisting the proposed plans for commercial relations. But

46 *Ibid.*, p. 364.   47 *Ibid.*, p. 366.   48 *Ibid.*, p. 368.
49 *Ibid.*, p. 378.

as he was not as able or as strong a character as the former Panchen, he was cautious about openly backing a measure that might possibly gain him enemies in the Chinese administration. For even though the Dalai Lama himself had no objections to having the Englishmen enter the country, the powers in actual control there did object.[50]

Turner, like Bogle, admitted that he had been very eager to do anything in his power to make his mission a success, and therefore had been extremely anxious to continue on to Lhasa to try to gain the goodwill of the officials there toward the English and obtain their permission for free intercourse between Tibet and Bengal. But he was prevented from doing so by considerations of the current state of the Lhasa Government, and by the advice of the Tashilhunpo Regent, who had strongly dissuaded him from making the attempt.[51] However, as a form of compensation, the Regent had promised to find out the thoughts and wishes of the Dalai Lama regarding relations with the English, and said he would communicate them directly to Hastings. These are of course the same tactics that the Sixth Panchen Lama had employed in the case of Bogle.

In regard to the larger aims of his mission, Turner said that whenever a regular intercourse became established between the agents of the Government of Bengal and the rulers of Tibet, he would consider it as a sure basis for relations with China from the interior of Asia. He felt that it would probably be by means of their Tibetan contacts that the English would find it possible to reach Peking.

As a step in this direction, Turner reported that he had obtained the Tashilhunpo Regent's promise to encourage all Indian merchants who might come to Tibet to trade on behalf of the Government of Bengal, and that Hastings' authority alone would be sufficient to secure them the

[50] *Ibid.*, p. 368.   [51] *Ibid.*, p. 373.

Regent's protection. The Regent further promised that he would grant free admission to Tibet to all Indian merchants that were recommended by Hastings. He would give them every assistance for carrying their goods from the Bhutan frontier (by corvée transport), and would assign them a place to stay and sell their wares, either in Tashilhunpo monastery itself or in the nearby town (Shigatse).[52]

Turner explained that he had not attempted to ask the Regent to write out such an agreement. Not only were such formalities almost unknown in Tibet, but his promises would only be valid during the minority of the young Panchen, and the moment the latter was admitted to office he could revoke them. Moreover, the Regent had no independent power to enforce a treaty of commerce in his own right, as he possessed all his authority as the representative of the young Lama. And even if the Regent had had power of his own, to have pressed him to conclude a treaty on these terms would have been to abandon the larger aim, which was ultimately to establish a trading station at Tashilhunpo under the supervision of an Englishman. Turner characterized this objective as "the most eligible and certain method of conducting the commercial interests of the Company on a respectable footing and with adequate success."[53] He took a dim view of the more usual policy of using Indian agents, as in this case they would be stationed so far away from anyone who could check or control their actions, and he felt that any benefits resulting from a trade conducted through them would be extremely precarious at best.[54]

In regard to Bhutan and its position on the trade route between Bengal and Tibet, Turner reported that since Bogle had settled the regulations for carrying the Company's trade through that country in 1775, and since the Deb Rajah had acknowledged to him that he still con-

<hr>

[52] *Ibid.*, p. 374.   [53] *Ibid.*, pp. 375-76.   [54] *Ibid.*, p. 375.

sidered that valid, it did not seem necessary to draw up another until the trade was established on a different footing.[55]

In short, from a diplomatic point of view, Turner's mission had not accomplished very much, beyond cementing already-existing relations with the rulers of Bhutan and Tashilhunpo. But he did obtain a clearer idea of the complex elements involved in Tibetan politics which the Company would have to learn to cope with if its efforts were to be crowned with success. And at the same time, his thorough investigations of Tibetan trade added a great deal to the Company's knowledge of Inner Asian commerce in general, as well as giving a better idea of what might be expected when trade relations with Tibet were eventually worked out. Turner's report on Tibetan trade was far more detailed and comprehensive than Bogle's had been.[56]

Turner introduced the subject of Tibetan trade by saying that the country had been the resort of merchants from time immemorial and necessity had developed a commerce that was only languidly conducted by a naturally lazy people. He felt, however, that once the Tibetans had become acquainted with the pleasures of luxury and the profits of commerce, they would be roused from their apathy and would feel the need for a higher standard of living.[57] One of the drawbacks to wider trade, he pointed out, was the fact that in Bhutan and Tibet the highest ruler of the state was the chief merchant, enjoying advantages far above ordinary traders because of his authority, and monopolizing all trade, except for a limited amount granted to a few of the highest officials who were allowed

55 *Ibid.*, p. 376.

56 That is, unless Bogle said considerably more in a list of principal articles of trade, with their prices and the cost of their transport, which he speaks of enclosing in his final report to Hastings (Markham, *ibid.*, p. 204), but which seems to have been lost.

57 Turner, pp. 368-69.

special privileges for trading in necessities. This suppressed emulation discouraged a natural development of trade.[58] As to the possible resources of Tibet which could be exchanged for manufactured products, Turner conceded that the soil was mostly beyond improving by cultivation and that the country gave a strong impression of poverty. But, he said, whatever the people lacked because of the poor soil, or the absence of skill in their artisans,[59] they had ample means of obtaining through the riches of the earth. For their mines and mineral resources were capable of opening to the Tibetans such inexhaustible sources of wealth that they could buy anything they needed, even though their wants were perforce numerous because of their inability to provide very much for themselves.[60]

Turner was apparently much more interested in the mineral products of Tibet than Bogle had been, and this subject was probably what most interested Hastings, also. For the latter had written, in one of his first references to Tibet, that the Tibetans were represented as "possessing at home the principal means of commerce, gold and silver in great abundance."[61] Then Bogle had reported that gold dust, along with musk, was one of the principal commodities with which the Tibetans paid for imports from Bengal, doubtless arousing his interest still more.

Turner elaborated somewhat, saying that the returns of Bengal's trade with Tibet had always been made in gold dust, silver, borax, and musk. (Bogle had not mentioned the silver or borax.) The value of these, Turner continued, was proportionate to the quantity in the market at any given time. The value of gold and silver, for example, var-

[58] *Ibid.*, p. 369.

[59] Turner uses the word artist, in its now obsolete sense of artisan. Whatever one might say about the deficiencies of their artisans and workmen, the better Tibetan artists are capable of turning out productions which would be considered works of art in any civilization.

[60] *Ibid.*, pp. 369-70.   [61] Markham, *ibid.*, p. 5.

ied exceedingly, depending on the amount of the former found in the Tibetan mines.[62] He reported that when he was in Tibet, a purse of gold dust sold for about seven rupees. But a few years before, the earth had cracked open during an extensive drought and such an abundance of gold was said to have been revealed that the price of a purse of it dropped to about three rupees.[63] Turner cannily remarks, however, that in spite of wide fluctuations in the profits of trade due to such differences in value, the balance would always be in favor of the foreign merchant.[64]

The silver which entered Bengal through the Tibetan trade was not actually mined in Tibet. Turner had mentioned silver bullion among the Tibetan imports from China,[65] and he remarked that Tashilhunpo carried on a profitable commerce with Lhasa, exchanging gold dust from Western Tibet for silver bullion from China.[66] However, he noted that their country had several lead mines which were totally neglected, commenting that, since lead is generally found to contain a variable amount of silver, he thought it likely that the lead ores of Tibet might be found to be rich in that metal. In which case it might prove to be very profitable to smelt these ores to obtain the silver, something the Tibetans had not yet learned to do for themselves.[67]

In reference to other minerals, Turner reported that the copper mines of Tibet furnished metal for casting the images and ornaments, etc., in the monasteries,[68] but that copper was apparently not exported. He said that the cinnabar which was mined in Tibet for use in red paints,

[62] Turner, p. 370.

[63] Turner (p. 370), speaks of a "pootree of gold dust," and defines "pootree," in note a, as meaning "bulse," which in turn means a small purse. He says that one of these sells for 21 "indermillees"; in note b, he says that an "indermillee" is worth about one third of a rupee.

[64] *Ibid.*, pp. 370-71.   [65] *Ibid.*, p. 381.   [66] *Ibid.*, p. 384.

[67] *Ibid.*, pp. 371-72.   [68] *Ibid.*, p. 372.

contained a large proportion of mercury,[69] but again the Tibetans did not know how to extract it. He discovered that the borax which the Tibetans sent down to Bengal, and also shipped to Bhutan, Nepal, and other parts of India, came from the bed of a lake about fifteen days' journey (to the west) from Tashilhunpo.[70] While in the same area, the Tibetans also obtained salt which they exported to Nepal and Bhutan.[71]

As to coinage, Turner reported that there was very little of it in circulation in Tibet, and what was used was of a base standard. This consisted of the silver coins of (pre-Gurkha) Nepal,[72] which were worth about a third of a rupee, and these were cut into halves, thirds, and quarters for lesser units. The Tibetans used this money for buying the simpler necessities of life. But for all the important transactions, payment was made in the form of small ingots of gold and silver, which were valued in proportion to the purity and specific gravity of the metal in them.[73]

Musk was such an important commodity in the trade with Bengal that Turner devoted considerable space in his narrative to the musk deer and its product, although in his actual report he only briefly mentioned it, with the comment that is usually adulterated.[74] In the former, he said that the musk deer was considered as the property of the state in Tibet, and was only hunted by permission of the Government. Accordingly, a great part of the musk passed through the hands of the high officials. All that bore the Regent's seal could be assumed to be of good quality.[75]

Lastly, Turner gives a short discussion of the Chinese trade with Tibet, since a knowledge of this would be

[69] *Ibid.*   [70] *Ibid.*, p. 371.   [71] *Ibid.*

[72] As we shall see in the next chapter, no coinage had been imported into Tibet from Nepal since the Gurkhas took over the country in the 1760's.

[73] *Ibid.*, p. 372. Compare Bogle's remarks on Tibetan currency, Markham, *ibid.*, p. 129.

[74] Turner, p. 371.   [75] *Ibid.*, p. 201.

important for the Company if Hastings succeeded in his plan of opening a back door for trade into China. He said this was carried on principally at Sining. The Tibetan merchants took to that city their cloth, gold dust, and a few commodities from Bengal, and exchanged them for tea, silver bullion, brocades and fruit. Turner mentions tea first with good reason, since it must have been the chief item in this trade. He had been told that in the territory of Tashi-lhunpo alone, the annual consumption of tea amounted to the value of five, or six hundred thousand rupees, which he explains was equivalent to sixty or seventy pounds sterling.[76] The Indian tea growers of the next century were to remember these figures. The possibility of entering that market gave them something to strive for.

Turner attached to his report a list of the usual articles of commerce between Tibet and the surrounding countries. This differs somewhat from Bogle's earlier information, and in itself it is very interesting for its picture of Inner Asia trade in the eighteenth century. It is summarized in Appendix D.

Warren Hastings was much pleased with Turner's reports and the outcome of his mission in general.[77] It must have seemed to him that there would soon be an ample outlet for the woolens and other manufactured goods that would once more be coming into India from abroad, now that peace with France had again rendered the seas safe for commerce.[78] And he doubtless looked forward to a flow of precious metals from the North to relieve Bengal's chronic currency problems. For a short time these dreams came true, though it was not until Hastings had returned

[76] *Ibid.*, pp. 372-73, and note on the latter. Turner also mentions (p. 373) that Chinese tea was taken on into Bhutan, from Tibet.

[77] Gleig, III, p. 161.

[78] See Turner's reassurance to the Regent of Tashilhunpo on pp. 276-77 of his book.

THE TOWN OF SHIGATSE, the trading post for Tashilhunpo, viewed from the fort. Photograph by Colonel C. S. Cutting

to England, so he was unable to enjoy directly the temporary success of his policy. Then, as we shall see, a series of diplomatic disasters brought a sudden and dramatic end to all his northern efforts.

CHAPTER V

THE BACKGROUND OF THE SINO-NEPALESE WAR

ABOUT the time Turner came back from Tibet, opposition to Hastings' rule in India began to grow in England.[1] This was partly due to machinations on the part of the friends of Lord Macartney, Governor of Madras, who greatly resented the controlling power of Hastings and his Bengal Council in Company affairs.[2] News of the attitude in England led Hastings to tender his resignation to the Court of Directors in a letter of January 1785,[3] and in the following month he left Calcutta for England,[4] leaving John Macpherson as acting Governor-general.[5]

It is conventionally said by writers on Anglo-Tibetan relations that when Warren Hastings left India, the plans for a northern trade, which he had conceived and initiated,

[1] See Gleig, III, 163-65ff.

[2] Lord Macartney's biography is given in *DNB*, XII, 404-6. See also John Barrow, *Some Account of the Public Life and a Selection from the Unpublished Writings of the Earl of Macartney* (London, 1807), and Helen H. Robbins, *Our First Ambassador to China* (London, 1908). Among other things, Macartney's friends are said to have circulated a report that Hastings had thrown off the English yoke and was reigning in Calcutta as an independent prince (Gleig, III, 165). For glimpses from the other side, of the bad feeling between Macartney and Hastings, see Barrow, I, 227-28 *et passim*, and Robbins, pp. 146ff.

[3] Quoted in Gleig, III, 231-32.

[4] Hastings left Calcutta on February 1st and sailed on the 6th. See Davies, p. 417.

[5] Macpherson had been the senior member on the Council, so he automatically succeeded to the post of Governor-general, pending the arrival of a new appointee from England. For his biography see *DNB*, XII, 711-12.

collapsed because of the lack of anyone with sufficient vision to continue them.[6] This is something of an oversimplification. Friendly relations with Tibet were carried on by the Company for a number of years, until a series of fateful circumstances caused their sudden and complete termination for over a century. But these catastrophes cannot exactly be blamed on the lethargy of Hastings' successors. There were other factors involved.

As an example of the continuance of Hastings' policy, soon after he left, in February 1785, Macpherson consented to let Purangir return to Tibet with dispatches for the Panchen Lama and the Regent of Tashilhunpo, previously given him by Hastings.[7] Purangir arrived at Tashilhunpo on the 8th of May.[8] On the following day, he had an audience with the Panchen Lama, who was attended by the Regent and Solpön Chenpo, and delivered the letters and presents he had brought for him.[9] On the second day, he had an audience with the Regent and delivered the dispatches to him, after which he visited Solpön Chenpo, the Lama's parents and others.[10] Turner, reporting the results of the mission to Macpherson, remarked that Purangir was received cordially by all, "for they had all long been accustomed to consider him as an agent of the Government of Bengal."[11] Apparently it never crossed Turner's mind that Purangir might have simultaneously been an agent of Tashilhunpo, which seems very probable.

Purangir reported that Tibet was at peace, and that in October 1784, the young Panchen, who was still not more than three years old,[12] had been formally installed in office, in the presence of envoys from China, the Dalai

---

[6] Davies, pp. 430-31, and Markham, *Narratives*, pp. xxi-xxii, lxxv.

[7] Turner, pp. 419-20.   [8] *Ibid.*, p. 420.   [9] *Ibid.*, p. 421.

[10] *Ibid.*, p. 422.

[11] *Ibid.*, pp. 422-23. Turner's report to Macdonald about Purangir's trip first appeared in *Asiatick Researches* (Calcutta, 1788), pp. 207-20.

[12] Turner, p. 427.

Lama and the Regent of Lhasa, with all their court, including the Kalons,[13] and one of the Chinese generals who was stationed at Lhasa with part of his troops.[14] Turner does not seem to have realized it, but this unusual pomp, and the presence of so many dignitaries from China and Lhasa, must have been an effort by Peking and the Dalai Lama's party to make clear their sovereignty over Tashilhunpo, which had been all but lost under the reign of the very popular Sixth Panchen. As one indication that such a policy existed, in their selection of a new Panchen, the leaders of the Church had carefully picked a first cousin of the Dalai Lama to fill the vacancy.[15]

Turner obtained from Purangir a very detailed account of the procession from Terpaling to Tashilhunpo, and the subsequent ceremonies, confirming his testimony and gaining some additional information from another gosain who was also present.[16]

In regard to the recently established commercial intercourse between Bengal and Tibet, Purangir told Turner that although he had returned to Tibet so soon after he had been there on the latter's mission, he found that he was not the first to arrive at Tashilhunpo from Bengal. Many merchants had already come with trade goods, and still others followed before he left that place.[17]

Purangir reported that he had heard no complaints of impediments to trade or loss of goods, and he concluded therefore that all the trade agents had found the same ease of entry that he had, and the same assistance in getting from the border to Tashilhunpo. The markets at Tashilhunpo, he reported, were well stocked with English and

[13] The Kalons, referred to as "the Culloong," are mentioned *ibid.*, p. 427.

[14] The rest of the notables are mentioned *ibid.*, pp. 423-24.

[15] The young Panchen's father was an uncle of the reigning Dalai Lama. *Ibid.*, p. 230.

[16] *Ibid.*, p. 423.   [17] *Ibid.*, p. 428.

104

Indian goods, but there was not so much of them as to lower the market values below the prices of the two or three years preceding. Meanwhile the traders from India found the rate of exchange greatly in their favor.[18]

Purangir also reported that in the course of frequent interviews with the Regent and his ministers, during his five months' stay at Tashilhunpo, he had found them heartily disposed to encourage the commercial intercourse established under Hastings' auspices. He said that the Regent regretted Hastings' departure as the loss of the first friend and ally he had become acquainted with in any foreign nation, and that he acknowledged Hastings as the original cause of opening the communication and beginning a correspondence between the governments of Bengal and Tibet.[19] However, although he, the Regent, had from the beginning been accustomed to dealing exclusively with Hastings' agents, and there had thus been a personal feeling involved, he would not terminate the connection now, even though an opportunity was offered. Turner reported, furthermore, that the Regent had learned to have a deep and sincere respect for the English integrity of character,[20] and as Purangir assured him, the Regent was apparently convinced that the British intentions involved no schemes of territorial ambition, but were confined merely to trade in objects of utility and curiosity. Accordingly, the Regent had expressed a desire to maintain friendly relations with Hastings' successor. To this end he determined to invite the new Governor-gen-

[18] *Ibid.*, pp. 428-29. As an example of the favorableness of the exchange, Purangir reported that a purse of gold dust that formerly sold for some seven rupees could now be obtained—with purer metal—for about six and a half; while an ingot of silver, formerly worth about 167 rupees, was now worth 150 (*ibid.*).

[19] By contrast see Chapter II, note 6.

[20] One inevitably wonders to what extent this sentiment ascribed to the Regent of Tashilhunpo was the product of Turner's own chauvinism, or of the diplomatic flattery of Purangir.

eral to join him in preserving between Tibet and Bengal the same commercial and diplomatic relations, for the benefit of both parties. Therefore, when Purangir left Tashilhunpo to return to Bengal, at the beginning of October, he brought with him letters from both the young Panchen Lama and the Regent to Mr. Macpherson.[21]

On his return to Calcutta, Purangir found to his dismay that a neighboring landlord had appropriated his lands at Ghusari, which he had left in charge of a young disciple.[22] But Turner at the end of his report called Macpherson's attention to this injustice, and succeeded in reestablishing Purangir's rights.[23] In due course, the property was restored to him, and he settled down at the monastery.[24] This does not mean, however, that Purangir ceased to work for the Government of Bengal. He seems to have undertaken one more diplomatic mission to Tibet, and according to the report of another gosain who went to Lhasa in 1793 (we shall discuss his mission more fully, below), his monastery at Ghusari served as a translation bureau for the government.[25]

Just about the time that Turner presented to Macpherson his report of Purangir's trip, in February 1786, Lord Charles Cornwallis was reluctantly accepting the post of Governor-general of India.[26] This had been offered to him four years before, in May 1782, when he was still a prisoner on parole of the Continental Congress as a result of his surrender at Yorktown, but he had refused it,[27] and

[21] These letters are quoted by Turner, pp. 430-31.

[22] *Ibid.*, pp. 431-32.   [23] *Ibid.*, pp. 431-33.

[24] He lived there until his death in 1795. See Bysack, "Notes on a Buddhist Monastery," pp. 89-90.

[25] See text, below, and note 124 for reference.

[26] See Charles Ross, *Correspondence of Charles, First Marquis Cornwallis* (London, 1859), I, 208. Lord Cornwallis's life appears in *DNB*, IV, 1159-66.

[27] Ross, I, 14, 136.

in the meantime Lord Macartney had also declined the post.[28]

When he came to India in September 1786, Cornwallis had much more power than Hastings had ever had. Not only did he hold the additional title of Commander-in-chief, making him the military as well as civil ruler of the Company's possessions in India, but he was also given the extraordinary power to act in all cases of emergency in direct opposition to the opinions of the Council, if that seemed necessary.[29] If Warren Hastings had enjoyed such powers, the history of his administration, and its tragic personal consequences, would have been materially altered.

Cornwallis needed all his power and prestige to clean up the appalling corruption within the Company's organization in India. For the first three years of his rule he was fully occupied with civil and military reforms,[30] after which, from 1790 to 1792, he was forced to take charge of the Company's military campaigns in the Second Mysore War.[31] Then, on his return, he was once more occupied with reform measures, until he left Bengal in August 1793.[32] All this internal activity might give the impression that his other preoccupations would have kept Cornwallis from continuing his policy of maintaining good relations with the Company's northern neighbors. We shall see, however, that he still had time to become involved in northern affairs, though he seems to have handled them somewhat differently than Hastings would have done.

Turner tells us that the affairs of Tibet—meaning its relations with Bengal—continued in a flourishing and prosperous state till the year 1792, when intelligence arrived that the Gurkhas had commenced hostilities against

[28] Robbins, p. 157.   [29] Ross, I, 208, 214.
[30] *Ibid.*, Chapter IX, 239ff.; *DNB*, IV, 1162.
[31] Ross, I, 462ff.; *DNB*, IV, 1162, 1163. Samuel Turner fought with Lord Cornwallis in this war; see *DNB*, XIX, 1282.
[32] *DNB*, IV, 1163.

the states of Tibet.[33] It is probably true that no real break between the Company and Tibet occurred until 1792; but in the meantime affairs in the north had been steadily deteriorating, and Gurkha invaders had begun to stir up trouble in Tibet considerably before that date.

Bogle reported how the conquest of Nepal by the Gurkhas had disrupted the old trade between India and Tibet by way of that country, and he also told how the Tibetans had been annoyed by the Gurkhas' aggressive tactics toward the Rajah of Sikkim.[34] In addition, the currency question had long been a bone of contention between the Gurkhas and the rulers of Tibet.

The Newari Rajahs of Nepal had minted coins for the Tibetans since the reign of Mahendra Malla, Rajah of Khatmandu, in the sixteenth century.[35] For a time Khatmandu seems to have had the monopoly on this, but later the Rajahs of the rival states of Patan and Bhatgaon also sent silver coins to Tibet,[36] though the name *mahendra-malli* continued to be used for all these coins.[37] Father Desideri, discussing the excessive amount of silver bullion in Tibet after the Chinese invasion of 1720, when the invading troops brought in ingots as currency, says that when the Tibetans sent this to Nepal to be changed into the money of the three Rajahs, the latter charged nothing, but gave them an equal weight of (alloyed) coins for the unadulterated silver, thus clearing an enormous profit.[38] Colonel Kirkpatrick, one of the first English authorities on

[33] Turner, p. 437.

[34] See Chapter II above, and Markham, *ibid.*, Chapter XV *passim*.

[35] See E. H. C. Walsh, "The Coinage of Tibet," *Memoirs of the Asiatic Society of Bengal*, II (Calcutta, 1907), 11, 18-19.

[36] See Colonel Kirkpatrick, *An Account of the Kingdom of Nepaul* (London, 1811), p. 217.

[37] Bogle used the term "mahendra-malli" (Markham, *ibid.*, p. 129, note 1), Turner uses "indermillee" (p. 372), while Kirkpatrick calls these coins "Mehnder-mulie" (p. 217), and Duncan calls them "Mehnder-mulli" (Kirkpatrick, p. 339).

[38] Desideri, pp. 167-68.

Nepal, said that the annual profit on silver coinage before the Gurkha Conquest had yielded Nepal 100,000 rupees.[39]

The last Newari rulers, especially Ranjit Malla, last Rajah of Bhatgaon, sent to Bhutan and Tibet such base coins as to cause a decrease of nearly one half of their value,[40] thus causing the Tibetans to lose faith in Nepalese currency. But they still continued to use it, as it was their only form of coinage, other payments being made in purses of gold dust or silver ingots, as Bogle and Turner explained.[41]

Because of the past profits to Nepal from this silver coinage, when the Gurkhas took over Nepal, their chieftain, Prithvi Narayan, as soon as he had established his authority in Nepal, tried to introduce his new coins into Tibet. Bogle tells us that to accomplish this he sent a deputation to Lhasa with a large sum in rupees struck in his name, and requested the sanction of the Government to circulate them throughout Tibet.[42]

According to Bogle, the Tibetan merchants, being aware of the Gurkha Rajah's bad faith, refused to accept his coinage, so the Lhasa government sent back to Prithvi Narayan the artful answer that they were willing to receive his coins provided that he would take back all the

[39] Kirkpatrick, p. 211. He uses the term "lack" for "a *lakh* of rupees."
[40] See Kirkpatrick, p. 339, and Markham, *ibid.*, p. 129, note 1.
[41] Markham, *ibid.*, pp. 128-29, Turner, p. 372. Staunton was so far misled by the general use of Nepalese silver coinage in Tibet, that he says, "In the vicissitudes of power so frequent in many parts of the East, Lhasa had been already once dependent upon Nepal; and the effigy of its Rajah was stamped, as paramount sovereign, upon the coin of Lhasa." (Staunton, II, 52-53.) This is wrong on several counts. Nepal had once been a dependency of Tibet (see Chapter I), but not vice versa; the Nepalese coins were used merely for convenience in Tibet, since the Tibetans had no mints of their own; and none of the coins from the three kingdoms had the portrait of a rajah, instead they had Buddhist and Hindu religious symbols—those from Khatmandu a sword, those from Bhatgaon a conch shell, and those of Patan a trident (see Markham, *ibid.*, p. 129, note 1).
[42] *Ibid.*, p. 129.

money of Nepal then in circulation in Tibet; a condition he could not possibly fulfill.[43] However, the official Nepalese version says that the Tibetan Government replied that the amount of base Nepalese silver coinage from the Newari rulers then in their country was very considerable, and that the suppression of it would cause their people great loss, consequently they could not agree to the introduction of pure coinage proposed by the Gurkha Rajah, but must desire that the Gurkhas would continue to supply them with adulterated coinage.[44] The latter condition sounds very unreasonable, and is probably intentionally so represented, since the Gurkhas were trying to prove that the Tibetans were thoroughly in the wrong in rejecting their overtures.

In any case, the old coinage still continued to pass, and by the time Bogle visited Tibet, since no more was being introduced, it had risen greatly above its former value, in proportion to the ingots of silver and purses of gold dust.[45] It was still being used at the time of Turner's visit, though he speaks of its very small quantity and base standard.[46]

According to the Nepalese official memorial, again, nine or ten years after the first negotiation, the Gurkhas once more sent an envoy proposing that since the Tibetan Government could not stop the circulation of the base silver coinage, they should at least establish a just rate of exchange between the base and the pure, so that the merchants of either country might stand on the same footing as formerly in their commercial transactions. The Tibetans absolutely refused to consider this, and directed that the base coinage and the pure should be considered as having the same value; as a result of which there was no trade between the two countries, and the circulation of Nepalese currency was alleged to have ceased in Tibet. Once more

[43] *Ibid.*   [44] Kirkpatrick, p. 339.   [45] Markham, *ibid.*, p. 129.
[46] Turner, p. 372.

the Nepalese proposed a conference to settle the matter in order to save the trade between the two countries, a proposal which the Nepalese memorial asserts was insolently rejected.[47]

Gurkha memorials have long had the reputation of being notoriously unreliable,[48] and no doubt some of this testimony was deliberately slanted to make their case seem very reasonable while causing the Tibetans to appear thoroughly in the wrong. But we can be sure that there must have been an element of truth in this. No doubt the wealth-hungry Gurkhas did make repeated attempts to get the Tibetans to accept their new coinage, because of the desire for the profits that would accrue to them from the transaction. And we can imagine that they were impatient and offended when the intended victims did not willingly submit to being fleeced.

Meanwhile, the cupidity and greed of the Gurkhas and their expectations of vast profits from Tibet must have been considerably heightened by the tales of great wealth in Further Tibet that were told them by Shamarpa Hutukhtu,[49] the younger brother of the sixth Panchen Lama, who fled to Nepal after the death of the Panchen and the accession to power of his other brother, Chungpa Hutukhtu, as Regent of Tashilhunpo.

[47] Kirkpatrick, pp. 339-40.

[48] See Cammann, "New Light on Huc and Gabet," *Far Eastern Quarterly*, I (1942), 355, text and note 39. While this refers to the memorials of a later Rajah of Nepal, the comments are applicable to Nepalese memorials in general, for which the Chinese had a supreme contempt.

[49] Shamarpa Hutukhtu is a form of title, rather than a proper name, the first word is Tibetan for "Red-cap lama" (see Koeppen, II, 226), while the second, as we have seen, means an Incarnation or a "Living Buddha." The implication of this name would seem to be that the Sixth Panchen Lama, himself the second highest Incarnation in Tibet, had two brothers who were also "Living Buddhas," Shamarpa and Chungpa, one of the Red sect and one of the Yellow; showing how it was possible for one family to obtain wide power in the Lama Church. In most Occidental accounts Shamarpa is called Sumhur Lama; in the Chinese records he appears as *Sha-ma-erh-pa*.

The reason for this flight is not directly specified in the English accounts, although Staunton—again following the report from Nepal—implies that he must have thought that his brother had been murdered and that danger threatened him as one of the late Panchen's relatives.[50] However, the actual facts seem to have been somewhat less sensational. It would seem that, having lost the protection of his exceptionally tolerant brother, the Sixth Panchen, he was not only mistreated by his brother the Regent but also suffered persecution as a Red-cap Lama.

The official Chinese records put full blame on the Regent, whom they seem to have regarded less highly than Turner did. According to them, Chungpa Hutukhtu was something of a miser, and when he returned to Tashilhunpo after the Panchen's death, he seized the latter's riches, and failed to distribute them according to the established custom, either to the monastery or the temples, or to the Tibetan soldiers. Furthermore, he rejected his younger brother, Shamarpa, and did not extend to him any kindness because he belonged to the Red Church. Whereupon the latter resentfully went and told the Gurkhas about the sealed treasures of Further Tibet, and the especially excessive wealth of Chungpa Hutukhtu.[51]

[50] Staunton, II, 52. However, Turner's French translator, Castéra, citing Staunton for the flight of Shamarpa, gave his opinion that "Sumhur Lama" was Turner's Regent, who had to flee to Nepal because his imprudence in showing the child Panchen to Turner had exposed himself to the resentment of the Emperor of China. Turner, *Ambassade au Thibet*, II, 214, translator's note.

[51] See the *Shêng wu chi*, 5.34b. The first section devoted to the Gurkha campaign in this book (5.34-39) has been translated, somewhat loosely, into French by Camille Imbault-Huart, "Histoire de la conquête du Népâl par les Chinois," *Journal Asiatique*, ser. 7, vol. XII (Paris, 1878), 348-77. Much later (in 1926) it was translated into English by H. S. Brunnert and printed in Landon's *Nepal*, II, 275-82. As the latter translation has many of the same mistakes as the former, we may suspect that Brunnert was merely translating the French translation, rather than the original Chinese, as represented.

The most important official account of the Gurkha War in Chinese, the very rare *Kuo-erh-k'o chi-lüeh*, has recently been acquired by the

Whatever the immediate reason for his flight, Shamarpa did go to the Gurkhas and succeeded in arousing their desire for the wealth of Tibet, with the result that they invaded Tibet for the first time in 1788.[52] The Chinese sources assert that the invaders used the pretext that the Tibetans had increased the customs duty on the salt exported to Nepal and refused to settle the old currency problem.[53] Meanwhile the Gurkhas officially claimed that they only took this measure after their appeal for a conference on trade and currency had been insultingly rejected, and their letters of protest to the Emperor of China, the Amban at Lhasa, the Panchen Lama, and the Changkya Hutukhtu,[54] had been returned unopened.[55] This, however, seems to imply more diplomatic formality than the parvenu Gurkhas were wont to employ.

Library of Congress. Quotations from it in English translation appear in Rockhill's slightly garbled account of the campaign in "Dalai Lamas," pp. 50-62. Many of the edicts referring to this war, and communications from the front, are preserved in the *Tung-hua hsü-lu*, Ch'ien-lung, chs. 108-18 (this source is hereafter abbreviated as *THHL*, CL) as well as in the *Kao-tsung Shun-huang-ti shih-lu* (*KTSL*).

[52] *THHL*, CL, 116.10b, and *KTSL*, 1410.5. This first Gurkha invasion of Tibet has generally been forgotten, or else ascribed to the year 1790, as stated in the *Shêng wu chi*, 5.34b, and *Eminent Chinese*, p. 254. It is recorded properly in the *Ch'ing-shih kao*, 530.9b. Diskalkar, partly due to a previous misunderstanding by Abdul Kadir Khan, gained the false impression that the first invasion had taken place in 1785 ("Tibeto-Nepalese War," p. 360) and expressed regret that the documents concerning it could not be traced (*ibid.* p. 381, note 4).

[53] *THHL*, CL, 116.10b, and *KTSL*, 1410.5. For the question of the customs dispute, see *THHL*, CL, 108.28-29ff., and *KTSL*, 1312.35-37.

[54] The English translation of the Nepalese memorial says "the Lamas of Diggercheh and Changkya," but Digarcha was the Nepalese name for Tashilhunpo; and in view of the exalted station of the other people to whom the letters were allegedly addressed, the "Sankia" Lama must have been the Sanskya Hutukhtu, Grand Lama of Peking.

[55] Kirkpatrick, p. 340. This Nepalese memorial on the causes of the war with Tibet does not mention Shamarpa, but he is referred to in the *Vansāvalī*, an official history of Nepal, which says that the Rajah Ran Bahadur Sahi (the ruthless grandson of Prithvi Narayan) sent for "Syamarpa Lama," and learned from him "the particulars of the northern country." See Daniel Wright (editor), *History of Nepal* (Cambridge, 1877), pp. 260-61.

The invading Gurkhas immediately occupied the Tibetan strongholds of Nilam, Jongka and Kirung, all especially important because they controlled passes and trade routes.[56] This caused great consternation in Tibet, and that autumn the Panchen Lama and his Regent sent two Moslem mullahs, from Kashmir, down to Calcutta to see the Governor-general, to tell him of their difficulties and ask his aid.

The two envoys, Mahomed Rejeb and Mahomed Walli, arrived at Rangpur on the 8th of December, and were interviewed by D. H. McDowell, who held Bogle's old post of Collector of Rangpur. The latter sent them on to Calcutta in haste the next day, as they requested, with a dispatch saying that they had told him that the Lama's dominions had recently been invaded by the Gurkhas, who had taken possession of several frontier forts and a large extent of territory, refusing to hear of any terms of peace unless the Lama consented to relinquish to them "all the gold produced in Tibet." In view of this he inferred that they had come to ask for English aid against the Gurkhas.[57]

Copies of the letters which the envoys brought to Calcutta have been preserved in the form of rather garbled translations from the original Persian. The first was ostensibly from the Panchen Lama, but since he was still very young it was probably actually written by the Regent; while the second, from the Regent himself, was merely a

[56] These places had been involved in the dispute over customs' taxes. See *THHL*, CL, 108.28-29, 54, and *KTSL*, 1312.35-37 and 1318.5. In the Chinese records they appear as Nieh-la-mu, Tsung-k'o, and Chi-lung, while the invaders are called the "*Pa-lê-pu* bandits." *Pa-lê-pu* is simply the Chinese way of writing the Tibetan word *Balbo* which means "Nepal," or "Nepalese."

[57] This letter is preserved in the India Office, Calcutta, as "Home Dept. Original Consultation no. 27 of Dec. 22nd, 1788," and is reproduced in Sarcar, "Intercourse of Bengal," pp. 126-27, as well as in Diskalkar, "Tibeto-Nepalese War," pp. 370-71.

polite note requesting the Governor-general to pay heed to the first one.[58]

The Panchen Lama's letter is a very important document because of the sidelights it gives on the state of mind of the invaded Tibetans. It begins with the usual diplomatic phrases, going on to mention that a long time had elapsed since the Panchen had heard from the Governor-general, which made him anxious, and that he hoped for some friendly letters.[59] Then it briefly summarizes the invasion of Nepal by the Gurkhas some twenty years before, as a prelude to the news that the latter, still unsatisfied, had invaded Tibetan territory during the preceding summer, massacring, and plundering many places, including one near Kuti that belonged to the Panchen Lama himself.

When the Chinese Ambans in Lhasa heard about all this, the Panchen continued, they had written to the Emperor of China, who would doubtless send troops. However, he himself was very much disturbed at the idea of Chinese soldiers coming to Tibet and the damage that they might do to his people. In order to avoid this, he wanted to make peace with the Gurkhas and was sending a petition to the Chinese Emperor requesting him not to send troops; but the Gurkha Rajah would not agree to peace and could not be trusted to keep his promises.

The Dalai Lama, he said, felt the same way about the situation, and had written to the "Rajah on the Jumna" (the puppet "Emperor" Shah Alam), asking him to become an enemy of the Gurkha Rajah and find means to destroy him. But he, the Panchen, did not feel that Shah Alam had any power, and for this reason he was writing to

[58] Diskalkar, "Tibeto-Nepalese War," nos. 3 (pp. 367-69) and 4 (pp. 369-70).

[59] The Lamas at Tashilhunpo were probably under the impression that Macpherson was still Governor-general, since they had not had any communication with Calcutta since before Cornwallis took over in 1786.

the English.[60] He thereupon requested that the Governor-general should send a large force against the Gurkha Rajah and annihilate him at least.

The Panchen went on to say that he would try to make peace with the Gurkhas, but if he should not succeed, then a large army would come from China to go to Nepal. Then, if the Gurkhas in desperation should call upon the English for assistance, he did not want the Governor-general to comply with their demand. Twice he repeated his requests that the English should either actively help him by sending an army against the Gurkhas or else aid him by not assisting the enemy.

Before closing he insisted on the need for secrecy, saying that if the Governor-general should decide to send troops into Nepal, he hoped that the latter would make out that he was acting on his own, and never mention the Panchen Lama's name or the fact that they had been corresponding. He wanted no stranger to know about his requests, he said, because he was going to write the Emperor of China that peace had been concluded with the Gurkha Rajah, in order to forestall the sending of troops from China. And if the Emperor of China should ever be informed of his correspondence with the Governor-general, it would bring ruin and destruction upon him.[61]

After some two months' deliberation, Lord Cornwallis responded very diplomatically.[62] First recapitulating the Panchen's letter to him, to show that he understood the situation in Tibet very well, he expressed his happiness at the renewal of their correspondence, hoping that it would

[60] Shah Alam, although heir to the Moghul Emperors, was only a puppet of the Mahrattas and actually had no power of his own, as the officials at Tashilhunpo seem to have learned through their Indian contacts.

[61] It is interesting to find the Panchen Lama so candid with the English in his frank admission of distrust of the Chinese and his plans regarding future policies.

[62] See Diskalkar, "Tibeto-Nepalese War," no. 6, pp. 371-74.

TASHILHUNPO MONASTERY, the seat of the Panchen Lamas. The taller buildings with Chinese roofs house the sacred tombs which were looted by the Gurkhas in 1781. Photograph by Colonel C. S. Cutting

continue for mutual exchange of news. He then went on to say that he had always considered the preservation of peace as his first object, and was therefore much concerned to hear that the Gurkha Rajah had wantonly and without provocation attacked the Panchen's dominions, and had had no hesitation in deciding not to help the Rajah. However, as to sending a large army against him, that would be impossible: first, because of the expense involved; secondly, because of the lack of provocation to the Company by the Gurkhas; and thirdly, because of the importance of not offending the Emperor of China by interfering between the Gurkhas and the Tibetans, who were under his protection. Cornwallis elaborated on the last point by carefully explaining the importance of the Company's sea trade with China, and the resulting necessity to avoid giving the Emperor any cause of displeasure by interfering without his request. "The great regard which he professes for you will always prevent me (from) affording any assistance to your enemies," said the Governor-general, "but the same motive must equally determine me against any interference in the concerns of your Government, which his regard for you will doubtless induce him to protect."

Then Cornwallis concluded his principal remarks by pointing out that there had not yet been any communication by land between the Emperor and the Company, and by suggesting that the Emperor should be told of the intimacy between the Panchen Lama and the Company. If this connection were made known to the Emperor, he said, he thought that the latter would not only be happy to hear it, but would be inclined to increase it, by making the Panchen Lama the channel through which to express his satisfaction in it. Great advantages would arise from such a communication with the Emperor, and the secrecy that was now maintained between the Panchen and himself would no longer be necessary.

Cornwallis' discussion of trade and the possibility of more open relations with Tibet following his declaration of neutrality was probably influenced by current Company policy. For meanwhile, at home in England, the question of how best to establish trade relations between the company and Tibet was still a live issue. In March 1786, probably on the basis of information gleaned from Warren Hastings after his return, the Directors declared that a very beneficial commerce with Tibet—both in Indian and British goods—ought to be practicable, and that from it Bengal would receive a much-needed supply of gold.[63]

A year later they wrote—apparently alluding to the results of Purangir's trip in 1785, news of which must have reached London in the meantime:

> The encouragement held out at Tibet by the Regent and his Ministers, who appear to entertain a very high respect for our national integrity of character, has made us sanguine in our expectations that a most beneficial commerce will very soon be established with that distant country, to the great advantage of the Bengal Provinces by a regular importation of bullion, and to the encouragement of the manufactures of Great Britain by increasing the vent for her commodities.

This must have reached Cornwallis sometime in 1788, shortly before he heard from the Panchen Lama; but meanwhile, the problem of opening Tibet to trade seems to have interested Lieutenant Colonel Charles Cathcart, who was asked by the English Government, in the spring of 1787, if he would care to serve as Ambassador on England's first embassy to China. For in his preliminary proposals to Henry Dundas, who was acting head of the Board

[63] See A. Aspinall, *Cornwallis in Bengal* (Manchester, 1931), p. 178. The quotation is from a Bengal Public Letter from Court, March 14th, 1786.

of Control for India, he said that he wanted to take with him as his private secretary Captain Alexander Agnew, and then if their reception in China was especially favorable, the latter could return to India by way of Tibet, taking proposals for the opening of trade relations between Tibet and Bengal.[64] The expedition sailed in December, but in June of the following year, as they were passing through the East Indies, Cathcart unexpectedly died, and the ship had to come back to England with nothing accomplished.[65]

But to return to the beleaguered Tibetans: when English help was obviously not forthcoming, and the soldiers from China proved timid and ineffective, since the Tibetans had no army of their own capable of dealing with the invaders, some of the Lhasa officials negotiated with the Gurkhas as the Panchen Lama had predicted they would. Early in 1789 one of the Kalons, named Danchin Banjur, and the Depön of Yutog, a Tibetan military officer, made an agreement with the Gurkhas through Shamarpa. They promised that in exchange for the recovery of the three border strongholds—Nilam, Jongka, and Kirung—and the return of the invading troops to Nepal, they would pay an annual tribute of three hundred Tibetan ingots of

[64] Lieutenant Colonel Cathcart had been Quartermaster-general to the Company's troops in Bengal, and had had long experience in the East, hence his choice for the post of ambassador. His letter in which these proposals appeared, dated June 20th, 1787, is preserved in the China files of the India Office, London, as "Cathcart Embassy, xc." See Pritchard, "Early Anglo-Chinese Relations," pp. 237-40. Alexander Agnew and the Tibetan project are mentioned on page 239. Dundas's reply to Cathcart, discussing the routes by which the proposed embassy might enter China, mentions the "newly discovered communication through Tibet from Bengal," but suggests that it seemed "too long and hazardous to be entered upon, as well as very doubtful in the result." See H. B. Morse, *The Chronicles of the East India Company Trading to China 1635-1834* (London, 1926), II, 162.

[65] Morse, *ibid.*, p. 156.

silver, which was equivalent to 9600 Chinese ounces of that metal.[66]

This agreement was connived at by the Manchu officials Pa-chung, O-hui, and Ch'êng-tê,[67] who had been sent by the Emperor of China to help expel the invaders. But they required an additional stipulation that the Gurkhas would immediately send a tribute mission to Peking, in order to give the impression that they were offering submission after a Chinese victory.[68]

The invaders thereupon withdrew from Tibet, the Tibetans duly paid the first installment of their tribute to Nepal, and the Gurkhas sent a tribute mission to Peking. The latter arrived at the Chinese capital in 1791, bringing tame elephants, "foreign horses," and an orchestra, as gifts to the Ch'ien-lung Emperor.

[66] *THHL*, CL, 114.29b and *KTSL*, 1391.8b. This document of December 15th, 1791, refers to the agreement in question as an event of "the year before last," making it clear that the negotiations took place in 1789, and not in 1790 as stated in the *Shêng wu chi*, 5.34, and *Eminent Chinese*, p. 254.

[67] The biography of O-hui is given in several sources in addition to the *Ch'ing-shih kao* (334.5b-6b), notably in the *Ch'ing-shih lieh-chüan*, 27.16b-21, which gives an excellent detailed account of the events in Tibet from 1788-1793. The life of Ch'êng-tê is given in *CSK*, 339.4b-5b. Pa-chung, who committed suicide to avoid punishment for crime, was otherwise too undistinguished to find a place in the national biographies. These men were all Manchus.

[68] As additional evidence that these events took place in 1789, and not in 1790 as usually asserted, the *Ch'ing-shih lieh-chüan* (27.20) says that in the ninth month of 1789, O-hui and his colleague sent back a report that a tribute mission was setting out from Nepal.

[89] Kuang-hsü *Hui-tien shih-li*, 985.14.

CHAPTER VI

THE CHINESE CAMPAIGN AGAINST THE GURKHAS AND ITS AFTERMATH

IN 1791, while the Nepalese tribute mission was in China, the Gurkha troops once more invaded Tibet in force. They were angered because the Tibetans had refused to pay another installment of their promised tribute, pointing out that the Dalai Lama had never formally agreed to the treaty. This time the invaders did not content themselves with occupying posts along the frontier. They marched right up through Further Tibet, capturing Shigatse and Tashilhunpo in October, and on the 28th of that month they thoroughly sacked the sacred monastery of the Panchen Lamas.[1] They looted chapels and temples as well as dwelling chambers, and pried off the jeweled ornaments atop the stupa-tombs of the deceased Panchens.[2] The riches must have been indescribable, since Tashilhunpo had managed to hold off the Jungarian Mongols when they sacked Lhasa in 1717-1720,[3] and the monastery contained the accumulated wealth of centuries of religious gifts and tribute.

Tashilhunpo might easily have been defended, but the Amban Pao-t'ai, instead of organizing resistance against the invaders, carried off the Dalai and Panchen Lamas to places of safety, and prepared to let the Gurkhas have Tibet without a battle.[4] Meanwhile, the considerable army

1 *THHL*, CL, 114.16; *KTSL*, 1388.16-17.
2 *THHL*, CL, 17b-18, 115.10; *KTSL*, 1388.22ff., 1400.6.
3 Rockhill, "Dalai Lamas," p. 39, note 1.
4 *THHL*, CL, 114.18ff.; *KTSL*, 1388.23ff.

of monks at Tashilhunpo, who did possess arms and could have defended it, simply abandoned the monastery.

According to the Chinese records, the Tashilhunpo monks claimed that they had consulted the goddess Marici, and that she had advised their giving up the monastery to the invaders.[5] The news that reached China specifically said that the lamas had consulted "an image" of the goddess Marici; but this seems to have been an error on the part of a Chinese official who was transcribing a report from Tibetan. Actually they probably asked the advice of the incarnation of that goddess, Dorje Phagmo, "the Thunderbolt-sow," whose residence is not very far from Tashilhunpo. For she ranked immediately behind the Dalai and Panchen Lamas, and in the absence of those two with their regents and the Ambans, she would have held supreme authority. In any case, the Court at Peking was disgusted at what they considered to be sheer reliance on superstition, when a little physical effort could have prevented a catastrophe.

When news of these disasters reached China, Pa-chung, one of the Chinese officials who should have punished the Gurkhas the first time instead of letting them off with a sizable tribute, realized his mistake and drowned himself. The other two generals, who had been equally implicated, took the opportunity to blame all on the dead man, knowing that their defence could not be properly questioned without the testimony which he could no longer give.[6] They were pardoned and sent out to attack the Gurkhas a second time.

In view of the emergency, the Ch'ien-lung Emperor summoned Fu-k'ang-an,[7] a noted Manchu official, to leave his post as Viceroy of the provinces of Kwangtung and

---

[5] *THHL*, CL, 114.20b; *KTSL*, 1389.8.

[6] *THHL*, CL, 115.1b, ff.; *KTSL*, 1394.10ff.

[7] The life of Fu-k'ang-an is given in *CSK*, 336.1-5, and in *Eminent Chinese*, pp. 253-55.

Kwangsi and proceed to Tibet, to drive out the Gurkhas for good.[8] From the beginning, the campaign was very well planned, under the direction of General A-kuei and other strategic advisers in Peking.[9] The army itself contained a number of different kinds of troops, illustrating the composition of the Manchu Empire at that time. Fuk'ang-an was a Court Manchu, but his second in command was Hai-lan-ch'a, a Solon tribesman from Northern Manchuria,[10] and the soldiers consisted of Daghor horsemen from the Manchu-Mongolian frontier, recently subjugated Chin-ch'uan mountaineers from Western Szechuan,[11] and cavalry from Kokonor, as well as troops recruited from the natives of Eastern Tibet.[12]

This army went into Tibet by two routes—from Kokonor by way of Sining, and from Szechuan via Tachienlu—reaching Central Tibet by forced marches in the winter of 1792.[13] The campaign was one of the most difficult in history[14]—far more of an achievement than Hannibal's

8 *THHL*, CL, 114.25-26b; *KTSL*, 1390.4b-6b.

9 See *Eminent Chinese*, p. 8.

10 The life of Hai-lan-ch'a is given in *CSK*, 337.1-6.

11 These Chin-ch'uan tribesmen had defied the armies of the Ch'ienlung Emperor from 1771-1776, and had been subdued by A-kuei, assisted by Fu-k'ang-an and others, in a most difficult mountain campaign, known as the Chin-ch'uan Rebellion. See *Eminent Chinese*, pp. 7-8. The Panchen Lama apparently told Bogle about this campaign, but the latter did not fully understand him (Markham, *Narratives*, pp. 135, 159). It was probably in recognition of the great ability of these tribesmen in mountain warfare that they were chosen to take part in this campaign.

12 For the organization of the army and general preparations, see *THHL*, CL, 114.25b ff.

13 *THHL*, CL, 114.25b-115-2b; *KTSL*, 1390.5-6b, 16-17b; 1391.8b-10b; 1394.10-11; 1396.2b-3b.

14 The story of the campaign itself can be found in *THHL*, CL, 114-15, and in the *Shêng wu chi*, 5.36-36b, and Imbault-Huart's translation of the same (pp. 364ff.). Turner gives a brief, rather inadequate account of it, pp. 437-41, and Duncan wrote a short, somewhat confused description of it while it was still in progress, September 4th, 1792 (Kirkpatrick, pp. 345-48). Markham's account of the whole war (*Narratives*, pp. lxxvi-vii) is highly inaccurate. He says that the Gurkhas invaded Tibet in 1792, and were defeated by a Chinese General named "Sund Fo" in that same

crossing of the Alps—and one of the costliest up to that time.[15] Probably it would not have succeeded so brilliantly if the transport system from Szechuan had not been especially well organized and very systematically carried out.[16] In addition, the planners and leaders showed remarkable ingenuity, as illustrated by their use of leather cannon for speedy transport.[17]

Fu-k'ang-an found the Gurkhas still in Tibet. They had been retreating rather slowly, weighed down with their loot from Tashilhunpo. He pursued them and defeated them repeatedly, in a remarkable series of battles under the worst of natural conditions, driving them back through the Himalayan passes into their own country.

Fast as the Chinese armies marched, the news of their coming seems to have preceded them, and the Gurkha Rajah was thrown into a panic. Just about the time of the first pitched battles in Tibet, which from the beginning were so disastrous for the Nepalese, he did a very unexpected, but quite natural, thing. He suddenly signed a commercial treaty with his old enemies, the English, after having stalled off their representative for some time.

Efforts had been made to obtain such a treaty, by the Company's Resident in Benares, Jonathan Duncan,[18]

---

year—without explaining how an army could have come all the way from China so quickly.

[15] See *Eminent Chinese*, II, 681.

[16] *Ibid.* According to this source, a complete statement of the expenses of this war was never submitted.

[17] Markham gives a Nepalese account about the cannons of the Chinese army having been made of leather. The Arsenal Museum in Khatmandu has two leathern cannon which may be survivors from this campaign, though they are said to have been captured from the Tibetans on a later occasion. (See Landon, *Nepal*, I, 262-63.) They are in shape like the European-type of cannon used in eighteenth century China, and are made of many layers of leather around a thin tube of iron. This seems to have been a special device perfected in this campaign for getting artillery over the Himalayan passes.

[18] See his biography in *DNB*, VI, 170. Later, on Cornwallis' recommendation, he became Governor of Bombay.

since soon after he had been appointed to his office in 1788. It was to his interest to improve trade with the North, and it is also possible that Cornwallis might have urged him to get on good terms with the Gurkhas after receiving the letters from Tashilhunpo in 1789. For it would doubtless have occurred to him that if the Nepalese were out to obtain "all the gold produced in Tibet," as the Panchen Lama's emissaries had told McDowell, it would be very profitable to be on trading relations with them.

Duncan's agent in Khatmandu was another Moslem mullah, Abdul Kadir Khan,[19] the man who later sent the report from Nepal which seems to have so impressed Staunton. He must have been waiting in the Gurkha capital for some time without success; but the threat of invading Chinese armies was able to achieve what persuasion ordinarily could not have accomplished, and on March 1st, 1792, the treaty was signed.[20] Its terms merely involved regulations for trade, and they sound completely innocuous from a diplomatic point of view, although as we shall see, there is a possibility that there were some additional verbal promises of aid to the Gurkhas. But even if there were no outside stipulations, doubtless the fact of having cemented relations of any kind with his powerful neighbors gave the now frightened Gurkha Rajah a comforting sense of having friends in case of need.

A few months later, when the pressure on the fleeing

[19] In the report as quoted by Diskalkar ("Tibeto-Nepalese War," p. 381), the translator calls him "Abdul Cawder Khan," and another document (*ibid.*, p. 386) spells his second name as "Cauder"; Kirkpatrick, p. 361, gives it correctly as Abdūl Kādir Khan, describing him as a Moulahvi, or Moslem holy man. It is interesting to note how the Company and the other nations with which it dealt made use of holy men, whether Moslem or Hindu, for diplomatic interchanges. Probably this was done because their religious connections were thought to insure them of more diplomatic immunity among potentially hostile peoples, as well as offering some guarantee of their trustworthiness as individuals.

[20] This Treaty of Commerce with Nepal is given in Aitchison XIV, 48-49. (1929 ed., 56-57).

Gurkhas had become still worse after numerous defeats in Tibet, the Rajah of Nepal wrote a letter to Lord Cornwallis, which reached Calcutta on August 22nd.[21] He began by recalling that he had written before to tell of occurrences in the North,[22] and not knowing whether or not his Lordship had returned to Calcutta (from the Mysore War) he was experiencing the utmost anxiety. He went on to say that the disputes which had arisen between himself and "the Rajah of Lhasa" had doubtless been represented by an envoy from Nepal some time before,[23] but this year the situation had become more serious because the Chinese Emperor's representative (Fu-k'ang-an) had come to Tibet. In this state of emergency, he asked that Cornwallis should send him ten cannon, along with ammunition for them, and ten young Europeans who would understand how to manage artillery.

About two weeks later a second letter arrived from Nepal.[24] Once more the Gurkha Rajah alluded to having repeatedly written to Lord Cornwallis about the disputes and warfare between himself and "the Rajah of Lhasa," and recalled his application for assistance in the form of "ten pieces of cannon and ten European Sergeants." In addition to these, he now wanted the Governor-general to issue an order to the Commanding Officer of the Company's garrison at Dinapur, requiring him to send two battalions of Europeans and two of sepoys, with military stores and a suitable number of guns, and promised to pay the expenses for these.

Along with the second letter to Cornwallis, came one from the Gurkha Rajah to Mr. Duncan, the Resident at

[21] Diskalkar, "Tibeto-Nepalese War," no. 9, pp. 377-78.
[22] Unfortunately no previous letters from the Gurkha Rajah have been located.
[23] This envoy was Dinanath Opadeah, who had been residing at Calcutta for some time as the Gurkha Rajah's agent. See Kirkpatrick, Introduction, p. viii.
[24] Diskalkar, op.cit., no. 10, pp. 378-79.

Benares, which the latter immediately forwarded to Calcutta.[25] This began by saying that the sender had already written to him about his disputes with the Tibetans, and continued:

> You, and the English in general, endeavor at the successful issue of the affairs of those with whom you enter into Engagements. On this account I have every confidence in the English Gentlemen and have written frequently for assistance. I request that immediately on the receipt of this letter, you will write to the Governor-general and send your letter by [the Gurkha envoy], so that the assistance required may arrive on time.

This makes one wonder whether perhaps Duncan had held out to the Rajah some hopes of assistance in his Tibetan campaign in exchange for the recent trade treaty which he had worked so hard to obtain; or whether Abdul Kadir Khan had offered indiscreet promises in an excess of zeal for his employer. No previous correspondence is available, so we cannot know.

Meanwhile, on the 3rd of August, Cornwallis had received a number of letters from Tibet,[26] apparently brought by Purangir.[27] Among them was one from Fuk'ang-an, written on March 31st, 1792. In this, he asked the ruler of the English—just as he asked the rulers of Bhutan and Sikkim, on the same occasion—as a neighbor of the Gurkhas, to help the Chinese punish the former for their unwarranted transgressions.[28] This was in the Man-

---

[25] *Ibid.*, no. 11, p. 379.

[26] A letter from the Dalai Lama has been twice published (see note 31, below), the others are referred to by Duncan in a reply to the Gurkha Rajah (Diskalkar, *ibid.*, p. 385) and in a report from Cornwallis and his aides to the Directors in London. (*Ibid.*, p. 392.)

[27] A later letter from the Panchen Lama mentions that these were transmitted through Purangir, who may have been in Tibet on another pilgrimage (*ibid.*, p. 395). See also note 72, below.

[28] *THHL*, CL, 115.6-6b, 9b; *KTSL*, 1398.11b-13b, 1400.7.

chu script, as were several of the other letters that arrived
at the same time (probably from the Ambans), and could
not immediately be read.[29] However, a letter from the Panchen Lama in Persian gave the substance of the rest,[30] and
Cornwallis managed to have translated a letter in Tibetan
from the Dalai Lama.[31] The latter told Cornwallis that the
Gurkha troops who had previously invaded his domains
had fled at the approach of a Chinese army. He warned
that the Gurkha Rajah would ask for English aid, and not
only urged Cornwallis not to aid the Rajah against China,
but further requested that if any fugitive Gurkha chieftains should fall into his hands, he should seize them, and
deliver them up to the Emperor of China, or at least prevent them from returning home.

On the 15th of September, Abdul Kadir Khan's report
from Nepal reached Calcutta, forwarded by Duncan.[32]
Although it was rather garbled in its narrative of past
events, this brought the latest news of the Gurkha War.
It reported that the Chinese had defeated the Nepalese
troops repeatedly, and that on the day of writing (September 4th), the Chinese Commander-in-chief was only
ten marches away from Khatmandu; the royal treasure had
been carried away to Mukwanpur for safekeeping, and
the Rajah was probably now there himself. Even if the
Company had considered helping the Gurkhas, it was now
too late.

[29] In the report to the Directors, Cornwallis says, "(These letters) were
written in the Mantchoux language (which is said to be the Tartar
language of the Emperor's Court) and we have not yet been able to
obtain translations of them." (*Ibid.*, p. 392.)

[30] The Panchen Lama's Persian letter was referred to by Cornwallis in
his report (*ibid.*), and by the Panchen Lama himself in a later letter
(Diskalkar, *ibid.*, p. 395).

[31] Diskalkar, *ibid.*, no. 8, pp. 375-76, and Kirkpatrick, pp. 348-49. In
the latter translation (p. 348) the Mohammedan year date for the first
Gurkha invasion of Tibet has been mis-rendered as 1789, instead of 1788.

[32] The translation from the Persian original is reproduced by Diskalkar, *ibid.*, no. 12, pp. 380-83, and summarized by Kirkpatrick, pp. 345-48.

That same day Cornwallis sent his reply to the Gurkha Rajah, acknowledging the two letters that had requested military aid. He carefully explained that the Company was anxious to remain on friendly terms with all the powers in India, particularly with those whose lands adjoined its own territories (as Nepal now did). Therefore, it was careful not to interfere in the disputes of others, except when wanton attack or considerations of self-defense made it necessary to do so. He pointed out that, in this case, it was especially necessary to adhere to this policy, because the Company had interests in China, and could not afford to send aid against a dependency of hers. He closed by offering to assist in mediation between the Rajah and his enemies, and promised that when the rains ended, he would depute an emissary to help settle the disagreement.[33]

Having decided on this tack, ten days later Cornwallis wrote to the Dalai Lama, acknowledging the receipt of the several letters. He admitted having heard from the Gurkha Rajah, but explained that, as the Company could not interfere in disputes between foreign powers except in cases of attack or self-defense, he had answered him accordingly. Cornwallis went on to say that, as a friendship had long subsisted between the Company and the Rajah of Nepal and between the Company and China, he was therefore now planning to send a man to help mediate the quarrel, as soon as the season permitted.[34] On the same day he sent similar letters to the Panchen Lama and to Fuk'ang-an.[35] Purangir was feeling ill and not up to venturing across the mountains in winter. So the letters were taken by his disciple, Daljit Gir.[36]

33 Diskalkar, ibid., no. 13, pp. 383-85, and Kirkpatrick, pp. 349-50.
34 Diskalkar, ibid., no. 15, pp. 387-89, and Kirkpatrick, pp. 351-52.
35 Kirkpatrick, p. 352, note.
36 We know this from the Panchen Lama's reply, which speaks of receiving Cornwallis' letter through "Daljit Gosain" because of Purangir's indisposition (ibid., pp. 395-96), and from a Chinese memorial which will be discussed at the end of the chapter. Dajit Gir succeeded Purangir as

By the 30th of September, the weather had begun to clear, so Cornwallis sent Captain William Kirkpatrick of the Bengal Infantry to Nepal as his envoy to assist in mediation.[37] He gave him a letter to the Rajah of Nepal, and a second for his Minister, the Regent and *de facto* ruler, expressing his hopes for the restoration of peace between Nepal and Tibet, and an increase of the benefits expected from the commercial intercourse established between the subjects of the Company and the people of Nepal.[38]

On the 15th of October, Cornwallis sent additional notes to the Dalai and Panchen Lamas, Fu-k'ang-an, and the Regent of Tashilhunpo, informing them that his representative was leaving for Nepal to assist in restoring peace.[39]

After all these advance announcements, Kirkpatrick found himself in a rather ridiculous position when his mission finally reached Nepal in February. For he found that the war had been over for several months, and the terms had already been settled.

Events in the North had moved briskly. Shortly after Abdul Kadir Khan sent his report from Nepal, Fu-k'ang-an drove the Gurkhas into the very valley of Khatmandu. He gave them a final, thoroughly decisive defeat at Nawakot,[40] only twenty miles from their capital city. The Gurkhas were desperate, fearing the complete seizure of their country, and immediately sued for peace. Fu-k'ang-an decided to accept their submission without going on to

head of the monastery at Ghusari. See Bysack, "Notes on a Buddhist Monastery," p. 91.

[37] Cornwallis obviously did not wait for a favorable reply from the Gurkha Rajah as implied in Kirkpatrick (introduction, p. viii), which says, "His offer, though falling short of what was desired, and perhaps expected, by the Nepaul Regent, was, nevertheless, accepted; and Captain Kirkpatrick was in consequence appointed. . . . "

[38] Kirkpatrick, p. 353. [39] *Ibid.*, p. 354.

[40] Though spelled Nawakot on modern maps, this also appears in histories as "Nayakot" (Markham, *Narratives*, p. lxxvii), and "Noakote" (Kirkpatrick, p. 347), and other related variants.

sack Khatmandu itself, because the Rajah of Nepal had already fled with his treasury, as had been reported, and meanwhile the season for crossing the passes back into Tibet was rapidly drawing to a close. He did not want to be cut off from his supplies in hostile territory.[41]

According to the conditions demanded of them, the Gurkhas returned all the treasures they had looted from Tashilhunpo, and handed over to the victors the Kalon, Danchin Banjur, together with Shamarpa's Tibetan wife and followers, as well as the body of Shamarpa himself, since the latter had taken poison to avoid falling into the hands of the Chinese alive.[42] In addition they promised to send a regular tribute to Peking. In regard to the latter, it was stipulated that Nepal's tribute status was to be like that of various other "dependents" of China, such as Korea, Annam, Siam, and Burma,[43] and that the tribute gifts were to consist of elephants, horses and peacocks, ivory, rhinoceros horns, peacock plumes, and other unspecified items; to be offered every five years.[44]

Fu-k'ang-an remained in Tibet for a time, arranging

[41] The official history of Nepal characteristically has a very different tale to tell. According to this, a Gurkha army cut the Chinese army to pieces on a hill north of Nawakot; and afterwards the Chinese Emperor, thinking it better to live in friendship with the Gurkhas, made peace with them (Wright, *History of Nepal*, pp. 260-61). A more temperate Nepalese view considers the campaign to have been a deadlock, and the resulting treaty sufficiently ambiguous to please both sides. See The Sirdar Ikbal Ali Shah, *Nepal: the Home of the Gods* (London, 1938), p. 45. This latter view seems to be that held by Landon (*Nepal*, I, 68-69), while Sylvain Lévi admits that the Gurkhas were decisively vanquished (*Le Népal*, I, 179-80).

[42] *THHL*, CL, 116.11b, and *KTSL*, 1411.10b-11. The death of Shamarpa is reported in *THHL*, CL, 116.3b-4, and *KTSL*, 1410.5-7. Imbault-Huart (p. 371) thought Danchin and Banjur were the names of two people.

[43] *THHL*, CL, 116.12b and *KTSL*, 1411.14b.

[44] See the Kuang-hsü *Hui-tien*, 67.13b. The last payment was made in 1908, only three years before the fall of the Ch'ing Dynasty (see Landon, *Nepal*, II, 102-3).

for the strengthening of Chinese control over the country.[45] For the Court at Peking wanted to insure the fact that they would never have to send another such costly expedition into Tibet. Among other things, he had the southern frontier of Tibet, where it bordered on Bhutan, Sikkim and Nepal, carefully marked off by monuments made of piled stones, called öbös.[46] As a sequel of the victory and this border settlement, the Rajah of Sikkim offered to become a vassal of China in return for the protection of Sikkim itself and the Chumbi Valley against the Nepalese.[47] The Gurkhas retaliated by attempting to claim these lands by right of past conquests, but the Chinese ignored their memorial on this subject.[48]

The Chinese also put an end to the Gurkha importunities about the acceptance of their Nepalese currency in Tibet, by insisting that the Tibetans should have their òwn silver coins, with Chinese, or Chinese and Tibetan, inscriptions. Even the importation of coinage from Bhutan was forbidden. All Gurkhas were strictly forbidden to enter Tibet, and Tibetans were forbidden to go down to Nepal without permission.[49]

We have been unable to discover the ultimate bodily fate of the Kalon, Danchin Banjur, or that of the Regent

[45] Sir Charles Bell, speaking of Tibet in the eighteenth century, before the Nepal Invasion, says, "It seems clear that, in spite of the decrees that the Chinese Emperor issued, and the seals of office that he bestowed, the actual control of China in Tibetan affairs was spasmodic, and limited to the neighborhoods of their garrisons" (Religion of Tibet, p. 154).

[46] THHL, CL, 116.14b, 18b, ff., and KTSL, 1411.24b, 1412.25ff. The use of öbös as boundary markers was nothing new. Bogle, describing his entrance into Tibet in 1774, says that on reaching the top of the pass leading to Phari, he and his companions found six heaps of stones with banners, serving to mark the boundary between Bhutan and Tibet (Markham, Narratives, p. 67).

[47] KTSL, 1423.20-20b.   [48] THHL, CL, 118.9b-11.

[49] THHL, CL, 116.12b-13, 37b, and KTSL, 1411.13b-15, 1418.9b-10. For further reference to the Chinese solution of the Tibetan currency problem, see the Kuang-hsü Hui-tien shih-li, 980.11-14, and E. H. C. Walsh, "The Coinage of Tibet," pp. 11-23. Unfortunately the latter has numerous errors that diminish its value.

Chungpa Hutukhtu, who was blamed by the Chinese for helping to bring on the war and then for failing to defend Tashilhunpo and the young Panchen Lama, his ward, against the Gurkha invaders.[50] However, all the wealth and property of these two, along with Shamarpa's possessions, were confiscated and turned over to the Dalai Lama, who was requested to use some of the proceeds to pay the Tibetan soldiers from Chamdo and elsewhere in Eastern Tibet who had taken part in the recent campaign.[51] The combined treasure is said to have been worth more than 64,000 ounces of silver, while the annual rent for the lands that were confiscated was computed at more than 7100 ounces of silver.[52]

As another aspect of the Chinese scheme to obtain complete control over Tibet, it was announced that the Dalai and Panchen Lamas and the Kalons could no longer act independently of the Chinese Viceroy. They would be obliged to consult the Amban on all points, and he would hold the final authority.[53] Even the selection of Lama reincarnations was henceforth to be controlled by the Ambans, who were instructed to superintend the drawing of lots from a "golden *bumpa* vase," instead of permitting the usual prearranged choice of boys from prominent families or powerful factions in Mongolia or Tibet.[54] By these measures, the

---

[50] As early as November 1788, soon after the news of the first Gurkha invasion of Tibet reached Peking, an imperial edict censured Chungpa Hutukhtu for his dealings with the "Outer Barbarian tribes." This expression potentially included both the English and the Indians. See *THHL*, CL, 108.35.

[51] *THHL*, CL, 116.19, 37-37b; 118.1-2, and *KTSL*, 1412.27-27b, 1418.8-10, and 1432.1b ff.

[52] *THHL*, CL, 118.1, and *KTSL*, 1432.1b.

[53] *THHL*, CL, 116.14-14b *et passim*, and *KTSL*, 1411.24-24b. As far back as January 1791, an imperial edict had announced the intention of curtailing the powers of the Grand Lamas and the Kalons, in favor of the Amban, after Fu-k'ang-an had straightened out the situation in Tibet. See *THHL*, CL, 114.33b-34b.

[54] The famous Reincarnation Edict of April 25th, 1793, is quoted in *THHL*, CL, 117.11-15, as well as in *KTSL*, 1424.23b-32. Rockhill gives a

Manchu Emperor of China now became the complete master of Tibet. And Tibet in turn became a definite part of the Manchu Empire, rather than a vague, outer dependency as it had been for the previous seventy-odd years.[55] To emphasize this, a new commemorative tablet was erected in Lhasa.[56]

The strengthening of Manchu supremacy in Tibet itself boded ill for English ambitions toward dealing and trading with the Tibetans independently. But in addition, the role of Cornwallis in the Gurkha War had lost him the respect of both victors and vanquished. Neither side appreciated his having avoided openly taking sides and then having offered to mediate when the war was already over.

To both the Gurkhas and the Chinese the proposal of mediation seemed foolish in itself. The Rajah of Nepal had apparently been confident—with or without reason—that he would receive military aid in time to defend his country. Thus, a mere offer to mediate, even if it had come in time was certainly no compensation. Arriving late, it only strengthened his sense of humiliation at the recent defeat and the strong terms imposed by his enemies. The attitude of the victors was more complex. In the first place, the

---

partial translation of it in "Dalai Lamas," pp. 55-57, citing an incorrect date ("February or March, 1793"). This measure had been discussed for some time before the edict was formally issued, see, for example, *THHL*, CL, 116.13b-14, 19b, 32b ff., etc. Incidentally, the Chinese expression "golden *bumpa* vase" is somewhat redundant, since *bum-pa* is the Tibetan word for a particular form of ritual vase.

[55] See note 90 for the status of Tibet before 1792, and Staunton, *Embassy*, II, 62, for the English realization that Tibet was now an integral part of China.

[56] The Gurkha Pacification Tablet, dated September 1793, was erected in front of the *Jo-kang*, the "Cathedral" of Lhasa. Its text is given in the *Hai-tsang pei-wen*, pp. 10-17b.

Another tablet with the Chien-lung Emperor's comments on this campaign, written in 1792, was set up in front of the Potala (*ibid.*, pp. 3-4b). See also *THHL*, CL, 116, 22b-23b, and *KTSL*, 1414.9ff. An atrocious translation of the latter one is presented by Sir Charles Bell, *Tibet, Past and Present*, pp. 275-78, and was republished, with a few corrections —but by no means enough—in Landon's *Nepal*, II, 272-74.

concept of mediation by a small neutral power was unfamiliar in the Far East. Except when a suzerain felt obliged to make peace between quarreling vassals, the victor in any war simply imposed his terms without outside interference. Mediation was especially unthinkable after the Chinese army had successfully avenged one of its vassals against an aggressive "tribe of bandits." Accordingly they considered the Company's Governor-general an ignorant and meddling barbarian for having suggested it. In the second place, as we shall see, the officers of the punitive army, notably Fu-k'ang-an himself, were suspicious that the Gurkhas might have been aided, or at least encouraged, from Bengal.[57] The various reactions soon became apparent.

The only friendly response to Cornwallis' letters announcing his proposal to mediate came from the Panchen Lama, who replied without delay.[58] He gave a fairly complete account of the war and its results. Then, in reference to the offer of mediation, he simply said that while the proposal gave him pleasure, there was no point in going to the trouble of sending an agent to the Gurkha Rajah, because now the latter had also become a dependent of the Emperor of China, and within the Empire there was no reason for dispute. He ended the letter with a request to keep up the friendly correspondence by letter and to write frequently.

In spite of the final words, this was the last letter ever received from the Panchen Lama. It does not seem likely, in view of later testimony, that the Lama could have sent it out before the censorship imposed by Fu-k'ang-an closed down on even the highest Lamas as described below. There-

[57] See text below, and references in note 65. However, as will later be emphasized, Fu-k'ang-an and the other Chinese officials did not necessarily think of the foreigners suspected of aiding the Gurkhas as being specifically English.

[58] Diskalkar, *ibid.*, no. 18, pp. 395-98.

fore it is interesting to speculate whether the Chinese authorities might have approved this as an easy way of answering the Governor-general's letters, since they doubtless had no intention of ever replying to it themselves.

When Lord Cornwallis heard from his envoy in Patna, en route to Nepal, that the Chinese had already defeated the Gurkhas and imposed terms on them, he replied that he thought it was still desirable for the mission to continue on. They could at least investigate the causes of the recent war, so that if the quarrel should break out again, the English would be able to judge the best way of mediating it.

In addition, Cornwallis drew up a list of other objectives for the mission and forwarded it to Kirkpatrick. The fifth objective was an investigation into the nature of the trade which the people of Nepal carried on with the natives of Tibet and Tartary, and an effort to discover whether any articles of British export could find a market in those channels.[59]

When he finally arrived in Nepal, in February 1793, Kirkpatrick found the Gurkhas very lukewarm toward him. One of the few favorable results of his mission was the information he brought back about the hitherto littleknown country of Nepal. This included a "Memorandum respecting the commerce of Nepaul," devoted mainly to suggestions regarding a trade between Bengal and Tibet by way of that country, in response to Cornwallis' request.[60] In it, Kirkpatrick urged Tibet as a market for the woolen staples of Great Britain, and explained that the reasons why such a trade had not yet developed were due to the

[59] Ross, *Correspondence of Cornwallis*, II, 206. Lévi (*Le Népal*, I, 309) goes so far as to say that the essential object of the Kirkpatrick Mission was the opening of commercial relations between British India and Tibet by way of Nepal. But Cornwallis' list of objectives would tend to show that while this was certainly an important aim, it was apparently not the chief one.

[60] Kirkpatrick, pp. 371-79.

jealousy of the border states between Bengal and Tibet, and "their ignorance of the true principles and advantages of a free commerce." But he said in addition, that something should also be ascribed to the distrustful character of the Chinese, who had in late years rather openly assumed the entire government of Tibet, and blamed on them the failure of Hastings' attempts to open a free commercial intercourse with the Tibetans.[61] He proposed topics for another treaty of commerce with the Government of Nepal which would encourage a trade in English woolens with Tibet, and provide for native agents of the Company to be stationed at the chief points on the boundary of Nepal and Tibet.[62] He further suggested that, since the successful operation of the new treaty would depend very materially on the conduct of the Chinese Government in Tibet, it might be necessary to request the assistance of Lord Macartney, who was then at the Court of the Ch'ien-lung Emperor, on the first British Embassy to China.[63]

The proposed treaty with Nepal regarding Tibetan trade did not materialize. Not only were the Gurkhas not particularly friendly, having apparently concluded that they had been let down in the China affair, but also the outcome of the war had effectively demolished any trade relations that might have still remained between Nepal and Tibet after the first invasions.[64] Lastly, the suggestion of enlisting Lord Macartney's help was supremely ironical. For even if Macartney had intended to carry out Cathcart's uncompleted intentions of furthering the opening of trade relations between Tibet and Bengal by way of China, he could not even discuss the matter, for fear of diplomatic repercussions.

According to the testimony of the members of the Macartney Mission, while they were on their way to Peking

[61] *Ibid.*, p. 372.   [62] *Ibid.*, pp. 377-79.   [63] *Ibid.*, p. 377.
[64] See for example, Lévi, *Le Népal*, I, 310.

by boat up the Pei Ho, in the summer of 1793, they began to notice that they were being watched with an unexpected degree of jealousy and suspicion. On investigating the reason for this, they found that it was because of the orders of the Manchu official in charge of their journey. And the interpreter further discovered from conversation with the mandarins accompanying them, that the English were suspected of having given aid to the Gurkhas in the recent war.[65] Macartney, according to this story, having heard nothing about the campaign against Nepal, was much puzzled by the whole matter, and accomplished diplomat though he was, was somewhat at a loss how to proceed about it.[66] When he met Fu-k'ang-an, newly returned from Tibet, in Jehol that autumn, the latter behaved very rudely. Macartney did not ascribe this to the Tibetan affairs at the time,[67] but later he blamed the relative lack of success of his mission in some part on Fu-k'ang-an's suspicion that the English had aided the Gurkhas.[68] In a letter to Dundas in England, he forwarded a recommendation that another British envoy should be sent to make it clear that this had not been the case.[69]

[65] See Macartney, "Journal of an Embassy to the Emperor of China," in Barrow, ii, 203-4; Staunton, ii, 48-49ff.; and Pritchard, "The Crucial Years," p. 332.

[66] Staunton (ii, 50) says that it was only after Macartney's arrival in Canton, in the following year, that he learned by dispatches from England and Calcutta "what were the circumstances that led to so groundless an assertion."

[67] Macartney (Barrow, ii, 267-68) describes Fu-k'ang-an's deportment as having been "formal and repulsive," and suggests that while at Canton he might have met with some unintentional slight (from a foreigner), or "what is more probable, he may have remarked . . . and felt with regret and indignation that superiority which wherever Englishmen go they cannot conceal from the most indifferent observer." See also Staunton, pp. 246-47.

[68] See Pritchard, pp. 360, 380, and note 70 below.

[69] See *ibid.*, p. 360. Macartney explained in this letter to Dundas that he had satisfied Ch'ang-ling, Viceroy of Kwangtung and Kwangsi (Pritchard misspells his name) that Fu-k'ang-an had been disseminating falsehoods about English activity in Tibet, and that the former had sug-

It has been suggested that Lord Macartney exaggerated the Tibetan issue in order to account for his comparative failure, and indeed this seems quite convincing.[70] It is true that Cornwallis' letters to Tibet saying that the Company had long been friends with the Gurkhas, who had been causing so much trouble, could only have increased Fu-k'ang-an's distrust of foreigners in general, which he had apparently developed while serving as Viceroy in the Canton region. But it is by no means clear that he thought of the English specifically as the offenders. The *rulers of Bengal* were of course totally discredited with the Gurkhas, the Chinese and the Tibetans, and this feeling was inevitably transmitted to the satellite countries such as Bhutan. But all these nations thought of the masters of Bengal only as the foreign people who ruled from Calcutta, and who were vassals of the Moghul Emperor at Delhi— not as Englishmen.

The latter fact emerges from a report to Peking by Fu-k'ang-an and one of his fellow-officials from China, dated April 18th, 1793.[71] This says that when Cornwallis' letters from Calcutta, for the Dalai and Panchen Lamas and for Fu-k'ang-an himself, reached Lhasa two days before, they carefully questioned Daljit Gir, the gosain

---

gested that an explanation of the real state of England's connection with Tibetan affairs might be the subject of another letter from the King of England or the work of a later envoy.

[70] Pritchard is skeptical about Macartney's remarks concerning Fu-k'ang-an and the Nepal-Tibetan affair, and says (pp. 380-81) that the Ambassador, who had been steeped in the traditions of European diplomacy, when he was faced with ill success, had to find a reason for it in some special occurrence which caused the Chinese to be suspicious and jealous of the English; and that he found this in the Tibetan affair and in the progress of the British power in India, as well as in the slanders and intrigues of nations or persons likely to be injured by the success of his mission.

[71] This letter has apparently been preserved only in the *Kuo-erh-k'o chi-lüeh*, 51.3-9.

who had brought them.[72] In forwarding his testimony, they speak of the English in India, throughout, as *p'i-lêng* (from the Tibetan *phi-ling*, "foreigners"),[73] and Cornwallis is referred to as "the headman, Kuo-na-erh" (from the English word "Governor").

The report says, by way of explanation:

We humbly report as the result of investigations that the lands of the Moghul Emperor at Delhi are the most extensive of all the countries of India, and his vassals are very numerous. Calcutta is the largest of the Emperor's dependencies. It adjoins the southern boundary of the Gurkhas and is the extreme frontier of our outer borders. The barbarian people who live there trade at Canton, and we are under the im-

[72] The Chinese text transcribes Daljit Gir's name as Ta-chi-ko-li. It also speaks of his "uncle," Su-na-ko-li, who had delivered the original letters from the Dalai and Panchen Lamas to Calcutta, and said that he now lay ill among the *peling* (see next note). From the Panchen Lama's last letter (Diskalkar, "Tibeto-Nepalese War," p. 796) we know that Purangir had been the bearer of the original letters, and had been prevented by illness from returning with the replies, so he must have been the Su-na-ko-li referred to. This odd Chinese transcription of his name is obviously based on an alternative name, Suryagiri, by which he was known to the Tibetans. The brief Tibetan notice of his visit to Tashilhunpo in 1785 refers to him by this second name. See L. Petech, "Missions," p. 346.

[73] The Tibetan word *phi-ling*, often anglicized as "peling," means "foreign," and as a noun, usually with the suffix *-pa*, "foreigner," or more specifically, an Englishman from India. It seems to have been derived through the Indian expression *feringhi*, from the Persian *firingi*, "Frank." See B. Laufer "Loan-words in Tibetan," *T'oung Pao*, new series, xvii (1916), p. 482, no. 141, and further comments by Petech, "Missions," p. 334, note 1.

There is ample evidence to suggest that the Chinese did not know what *p'i-lêng* meant, and merely considered it as the name of a people and their nation, without realizing that it referred to the English, until at least the mid-1840's. Their failure to understand its true meaning in Nepalese and Tibetan documents caused the Chinese Court to reject an offer from the Gurkha Rajah in 1840, that he should raid the English possessions in India, while the English were attacking China in the First Opium War. See Imbault-Huart, "Un épisode des relations diplomatiques de la Chine avec le Népal en 1842," *Revue de l'Extrême Orient*, iii (Paris, 1887), 8-14.

pression that they are connected with the people from the countries of the West (Europe). When we, Fu-k'ang-an and Sun Shih-i, were in Canton, we did not know that there was a Calcutta tribe, nor had we any certain knowledge of their name, or from what part of the world they came. . . .[74]

Daljit Gir told them that the gosains had a Buddhist temple not far from the "headman's" fort (Fort William), and that every day one of them was on duty at the fort to translate official documents sent from Tibet. This provides specific evidence that Purangir's temple at Ghusari served a definite diplomatic function. Because of his duties in this connection, the messenger was able to give the officials from China full details about the Gurkha Rajah's requests for aid from the Governor-general, and the latter's attempts to maintain neutrality and secure peace.[75]

On the whole, this memorial was not too unfavorable toward the "p'i-lêng people," but it closes by saying that the Dalai and Panchen Lamas, and the Regent of Lhasa had sent letters to the Regent and the Solpön of Further Tibet, telling them not to correspond with the foreign barbarians, but to forward all letters to Lhasa to be answered by the Ambans; and that the memorialists had ordered the Dalai and Panchen Lamas to draft a joint reply to the letters from Calcutta, which they would read and approve before sending.[76] This is an example of how

[74] *Kuo-erh-k'o chi-lüeh*, 51.4.

[75] *Ibid.*, pp. 4-4b. The memorial refers to the gosains as "atsara lamas." The gosains were followers of the Hindu sage Sankara Acharya and *atsara* is a corruption of the title *Acharya*; while the title of lama is used here merely in the sense of "holy men," not implying any direct connection with the Tibetan priesthood. However, the Tibetans have tended to use the title of *Acharya* very loosely to refer to Hindu visitors in general; and they even applied it to Bogle in describing his first interview with the Panchen Lama. See Petech, "Missions," p. 341.

[76] *Ibid.*, p. 9. The Regent of Further Tibet referred to in this memorial must have been the successor to Chungpa, who had presumably been deposed for his crimes.

completely Tibetan foreign affairs were now controlled by officials from China.

Apparently this testimony of the gosain regarding the activities of Purangir's monastery impressed the Chinese officials adversely. For Turner wrote in 1793 that the Chinese had occupied Phari, the Tibetan border post on the road between Bhutan and Tibet, through which he and Bogle had entered that country, and that they had utterly prohibited the approach of strangers, even the peoples of Bengal and Hindustan. "A most violent prejudice," he wrote, "prevails even against the Hindu gosains, who are charged with treachery against their generous patrons by becoming guides and spies to the enemy, and have in consequence, it is said, been prescribed in their customary abode at Tashilhunpo."[77]

This, of course, prevented any more missions by Purangir. He stayed on at his monastery, and one night in the spring of 1795, he was murdered there by robbers who attacked the place in search of its rumored wealth.[78]

We have seen that Lord Macartney assumed that the bad feeling in China, presumably directed against foreigners in general as a result of the Nepal campaign, was specifically applied to the English, and had urged that a second envoy be sent to explain that they had not aided the Gurkhas. As a result of this, another letter from the King of England, with "tribute," was sent to Peking in 1795, and arrived early in the following year.[79] This told how the English had attacked the Gurkas in the rear, and

[77] Turner, pp. 441-42.

[78] Bysack, "Notes on a Buddhist Monastery," pp. 90-91. The date of Purangir's death is usually given as May 3rd, 1795, but this date inscribed on his tomb is actually only the date of its consecration (*ibid.*, p. 55), and not the date on which he was murdered, which was apparently sometime earlier.

[79] Macartney recommended that Staunton be sent on this expedition as the King's Minister to China, but he was attacked by paralysis and could not accept the appointment. See Pritchard, p. 372.

urged them to submit to the Chinese forces. The Ch'ien-lung Emperor wrote a coldly formal reply, explaining that his marshal, Fu-k'ang-an, had defeated the Gurkhas unaided, and that the English must somehow have gotten the wrong story about the war.[80]

In spite of the official sentiments expressed in this letter from the Emperor of China, a tradition seems to have unaccountably persisted in Chinese history that the British had attacked the Gurkhas from the rear, thus assisting the Chinese to subdue them.[81] But even this tradition of possible cooperation was insufficient to obtain concessions from China. Nothing the English could now do would suffice to make China agree to a trade between Tibet and Bengal.

The early efforts of the British to open Tibet had reached an impasse, and more than eighty years were to elapse before another official attempt would be made to penetrate the "Forbidden Land."

[80] See the Ch'ien-lung Emperor's letter of February 7th, 1796, quoted in *KTSL*, 1493.16b-18.

[81] *Shêng wu chi* 5.36, 37b, and Imbault-Huart, "Conquête du Népal," pp. 369-71, 374.

CHAPTER VII

CONCLUSION

WE SAW in the brief résumé of Tibetan history up to 1774, presented in Chapter I, that the Tibetans were historically a very diversified people, and were subject to many outside influences until the middle of the eighteenth century. Tibet did not begin to become a "forbidden land"—except for the natural obstacles to entry offered by the terrain—until the Manchu Emperors of China took steps to add it to their domains, after an army sent from China had conquered it in 1720. (Previously, Tibet had at times been a nominal tributary of China, but the Chinese had never had any direct control over it.) This process of Manchu imperial penetration was already well under way before the English became at all interested in Tibet. Thus, by the time the officials of the East India Company in Bengal had begun to consider opening trade relations with Tibet, the recent political events within the country—and on its southern border, in Nepal—had already combined to make it virtually a closed land, shut off from its previous connections with Bengal and Northern India. (A trade had long existed between Tibet and these regions, although the East India Company had apparently never taken any interest in it until the Gurkha conquest of Nepal had closed the main arteries.) In view of the Manchu imperial policies, then, the British efforts to extend their trade northward from Bengal into Tibet were bound to be slow and difficult, with many frustrations, even though the initial negotiations with the semi-autonomous Lama-ruler of Further Tibet seemed to offer some promise of eventual success.

We have noted also that the English came late onto the Tibetan scene in another sense; for that remote land had already become quite well-known in Europe through the travels and writings of other Europeans. While the earlier entrants had been missionaries, or in one or two cases, learned travelers, the motives that inspired the first Englishmen to enter Tibet were largely trade interests, and only secondarily the intellectual curiosity of their patron, Warren Hastings. Their first consideration was to try to arrange an extension of the Company's trade in Bengal with the countries to the north, in order to revive a strained economy in their possessions in Bengal. And secondly, they hoped to find some means of introducing British goods to China through her back door, so they could extend the Company's sale of manufactured goods from overseas. But even though these economic reasons were the direct stimulus in the search for new markets and new channels of trade in the North, the fact that they were sought in the Himalayan countries rather than elsewhere must have been due, at least in part, to the curiosity of Hastings regarding the almost legendary lands beyond the snowy mountains.

The men Hastings chose to be his representatives, Bogle and Turner, were both very young, but they were exceptionally well qualified for their appointments, being keen observers and capable diplomats; and while sharing the curiosity of their patron, they were eager to conform to local customs and thus won the good will of the Tibetans. It must be emphasized, however, that with all their capabilities, they would have been almost totally powerless to accomplish anything without the help, advice, and translating ability of the much-neglected Purangir. He was indeed one of the most remarkable men of his time and place, and deserves more recognition.

The journals of Bogle and Turner have been indispensable source materials for this episode in Anglo-Tibetan history. But they have too often been treated merely as engaging travel books, with unusual details about strange customs and the "mysterious" religion of the lamas. The writer has tried to read them from another point of view, with more attention to their economic and diplomatic observations, and this has brought to light their practical sides, which had previously been virtually unnoticed. For both were essentially practical-minded men when it was a question of advancing the Company's fortunes, and thereby their own.

In Bogle's narrative we clearly see the suspicions of the rulers of Bhutan and Tibet toward the expanding realm of the East India Company, and their jealousy toward the extension of its trade—except in the case of the Panchen Lama and the Regent of Tashilhunpo, who were apparently persuaded that more extensive trade from Bengal would enrich them, through their monopolies. The jealousy of the Chinese or Manchu officials toward the Company's ambitions for Tibetan trade is also apparent in his book, as in Turner's. However, after reviewing all the circumstances of the case, the writer feels unable to admit the validity of the long-held suspicion that the Panchen Lama was deliberately murdered while visiting Peking, in order to prevent him from having further negotiations with Warren Hastings that might lead to more concessions.

Turner's conclusions in general seem to be fairly similar to Bogle's, but in a number of instances his book contains valuable additional information, quite apart from all the new source material in the appendices. For example, his references to Russia's definite efforts to open commercial relations with Tibet—quite apart from the small trade in Russian goods conducted by the Kalmuks—are the first intimations of that rivalry to come, that was to have such drastic consequences for Tibet. For the fear that Russia would obtain excess influence and undue privileges in Tibet was the immediate excuse for the Younghusband Expedition that finally opened Tibet for the British in 1904.[1]

Turner's commercial reports not only augment those of Bogle in many particulars, but since his narrative was the only important source book on Tibet for at least seventy years after its publication, they had considerable influence in the nineteenth century. For instance, he discusses the importance of Chinese tea in Tibet, and the vast profits obtained from trade in it. And undoubtedly this discussion was one of the factors that stimulated the growth of the tea industry in Bengal and Assam, and other parts of Northern India, in the mid-nineteenth century. For it gave the planters extravagant notions of the profits that they would eventually reap from a tea trade with Tibet. Apropos of this, it was apparently the incessant demand of the tea-growing interests for political action to assist them in opening a market for their tea in Tibet that led to most of the British pressure on Tibet, and the resulting diplomatic incidents from the 1870's until after the turn of the century.[2]

[1] The English accounts usually give the impression that the threat of Russian penetration into Tibet was the only reason for the Younghusband Expedition to Lhasa in 1903-1904. But Colonel Younghusband himself stated that the primary objective of his mission when it was originally dispatched was to secure facilities for trade with Tibet. See Sir Francis Younghusband, *India and Tibet* (London, 1910), p. 259. A careful study of the background of this mission, moreover, would lead one to conclude that the primary object was never altered, and the potential threat of Russia might well have been exaggerated to justify taking extraordinarily high-handed measures that it would otherwise have been impossible to justify.

[2] For some years the writer has been gathering material for a monograph on the Indian tea industry, and its importance in the later ,English efforts to open Tibet. But this study, which bids fair to reach book length, is beyond the scope of the present subject.

Turner's report on gold in Tibet probably also contributed to the great interest in the Tibetan gold fields throughout the following century, when the Indian Government even deputed some of its native spies to spend considerable time trying to determine their extent.[3] The idea of Tibet as a source of gold of course antedated Turner's testimony, but his was the first specific account of Tibetan gold resources, and his remarks were obviously read and digested for a long time.

The fifth and sixth chapters traced the steps leading to the enforced culmination of the early English efforts to open Tibet. These form a series of events on which there has been much conflicting, and misleading testimony in the past. Just as internal economic conditions in the Company's possessions in Bengal had played an important part in causing the first attempts to open Tibet to English trade, internal economic conditions of another type were instrumental in putting an end to these attempts. For Hastings' successors were preoccupied with efforts to put their immediate house in order, and place the Company's possessions in India on a more paying basis. Not only did this occupy most of their time that might have been devoted to planning foreign ventures, but insofar as their measures were successful, they lessened the need for further markets in the north. In addition, Cornwallis' absence on the military campaign in Southern India prevented him from giving due personal attention to the problems of the Northern nations and the best ways of handling them, at a time when skillful diplomacy was essential.

However, even if Cornwallis had been a little more careful in his diplomatic dealings with Nepal and Tibet, it is doubtful if he could have accomplished much more toward opening Tibet to trade, or even toward keeping open the

[3] See *The Times*, London, Feb. 17th, 1869, p. 4, and Feb. 24th, 1870, p. 4.

existing trade channels. For the Gurkha Campaign gave the Ch'ien-lung Emperor the perfect excuse to gain complete control over the Government of Tibet—a thing he had probably hesitated to do earlier, lest he might run the risk of offending the spiritual subjects of the Dalai and Panchen Lamas in Mongolia and his other possessions. And once the Emperor had this power, it is only natural that he would have taken steps to enforce the Manchu policy of exclusion that had kept China itself—with the exception of one port—closed to the foreign traders. The historical process, of which we saw the opening phases in Chapter I, was now completed, and Tibet had become an integral part of the Chinese Empire. It seems rather ironical that Nepal and China, the two nations that had traditionally done most to civilize Tibet in its early historical period were jointly the means of sealing it off from without, in such a way that it was enabled to keep its own distinctive culture intact during a period of fundamental changes in the surrounding nations.

The trade routes to Tibet through Nepal and Bhutan remained shut throughout the nineteenth century. This was partly due to the events of 1792 and their sequels, and partly because the rulers of those countries could not be forced to cooperate—even after several punitive expeditions against them. The only solution would have been to add these border states to the already unwieldy Indian Empire; but that the British could not afford to do. Therefore they concentrated on Sikkim, which was small and weak, gradually absorbing it. They had suffered it to exist as a buffer state between Nepal and Bhutan, until the latter nations had been taught that it was unprofitable to be belligerent and threaten the peace on the northern frontiers of India. By 1889, however, the Maharajah of Sikkim was compelled to accept a British adviser, and to all intents and purposes, what remained of this small nation became a part of British India. Having by this measure obtained direct access to the Chumbi Valley and Southern Tibet, the British no longer had to worry about possible routes through Bhutan and Nepal. Up to this time, however, the Government of India seemed to remember the conclusions of Bogle and Hastings, that occupation of Nepal and Bhutan was the only sure means of coercing their rulers, but that this would be more costly than it was worth. Nepal remained a troublemaker for a good part of the nineteenth century, waging two wars with the English and twice more challenging the Tibetans.[4]

The power of the Manchu Empire over Tibet gradually relaxed to some degree, during the course of the nineteenth century, allowing the Tibetans more power to make decisions for themselves. This was partially due to the gradual weakening of the Empire in China, under the ineffective successors of the Ch'ien-lung Emperor, who had inherited from him a treasury depleted by the excess luxuries of his court and by his spectacular military campaigns, like the one against Nepal.

But the relaxation of Manchu control in Tibet was in some measure more nominal than real, for reasons of diplomatic expediency. Thus, when the Chinese Court was pressed by the British to open Tibet, they could refer the question to the Tibetan authorities; while the latter could still appeal to the superior will of their overlord, the Emperor, and his representatives, the Ambans at Lhasa, as their forerunners had done in Hastings' time. This evasion of responsibility for diplomatic purposes finally exasperated certain British imperialists in India. One of them, Colonel Francis Younghusband, eventually fought his way from the Sikkim frontier all the way to Lhasa in search of

[4] In 1855-1856, the Gurkhas actually invaded Tibet. In 1884 they collected troops for an invasion, but did not cross the frontier when the Tibetans agreed to certain conditions without the necessity for using force.

some Tibetan official with whom he could negotiate on the question of better facilities for English trade with Tibet. This was in 1904, one hundred and thirty years after the first Englishman had entered Tibet for that very same purpose. It would seem to have been a confirmation of the original apprehensions of the Tibetans, that the English attempts to invade their privacy and establish relations with them, which began in violence with the expedition against Bhutan in 1773, should have ended in violence with the invasion and looting of their holy city.

In brief, we have seen that the foundations for the chief trends in later Anglo-Tibetan relations were laid in the eighteenth century, before Tibet was completely closed by the Manchus in 1793; and that economic factors played a larger part than is usually recognized in determining the progress of events in the early English efforts to open Tibet.

Appendices

APPENDIX A

THE PRELIMINARIES TO THE BHUTAN
EXPEDITION OF 1773

THE Company's war with Bhutan in 1773 is usually represented by British writers as having been provoked by
the Bhutanese raiding into Cooch Behar, which aggression
caused the company to send troops to rescue the Rajah of
Cooch Behar and punish the raiders.[1] Actually, the story
is more complicated, and less creditable to the English.

During a struggle for power between rival claimants to
the throne of the small state of Cooch Behar, one faction
invited in the Bhutanese to help them, while the Minister
of another pretender appealed to Warren Hastings, then
Governor of Bengal.[2] Although Hastings ostensibly entered the war for the altruistic motives of helping the
wronged ruler of a weak state to regain his rightful position, and to help punish some aggressive raiders, he pri-
vately admitted in correspondence that his purpose was to
gain possession of Cooch Behar for the Company—apart
from whatever he may have hoped to gain at the expense
of Bhutan.[3]

Furthermore, in April 1773, even before the Company's
troops set out for Bhutan, a treaty was signed by the said
Minister from Cooch Behar and by the President and
Council of the Company (Hastings and his associates), in

[1] See Turner, *Account of an Embassy*, Introduction, p. vii ff., and
Eden, "Report on the state of Bootan," pp. 1-3.
[2] See Aitchison, *A Collection of Treaties, etc.*, II, 189.
[3] Gleig, *Memoirs*, I, 279, 295-96.

155

which the latter, "from a love of justice and desire of assisting the distressed," agreed to send a force consisting of four companies of soldiers for the protection of the Rajah and his country against his enemies—for certain considerations. Under the first stipulation, the Rajah had to pay fifty thousand rupees immediately to the Company's representative at Rangpur; under the third, he had to acknowledge subjection to the English East India Company, upon his country being cleared of its enemies, and had to allow his country to be annexed to the province of Bengal; and under the fourth, he had to agree further to make over to the Company one half of the annual revenues of Cooch Behar forever.[4] For such a stake, the Company could afford to risk a few military losses.

[4] Aitchison, II, 189-90, 308.

/\/\/\/\/\/\/\/\/\

APPENDIX B

\/\/\/\/\/\/\/\/\/

THE PANCHEN LAMA'S FIRST LETTER TO WARREN HASTINGS[1]

THE affairs of this quarter flourish in every respect. I am employed night and day in prayers for the increase of your happiness and prosperity. Having been informed by travelers from your country [the gosains from Bengal] of your exalted fame and reputation, my heart like the blossom of spring abounds with satisfaction, gladness, and joy. Praise be to God that the star of your fortune is in its ascendant; praise be to Him that happiness and ease are the surrounding attendants of myself and [my] family.[2] Neither to molest nor persecute is my aim; it is even the characteristic of our sect to deprive ourselves of the necessary refreshment of sleep should an injury be done to a single individual. But I am informed you far surpass us in justice and humanity. May you ever adorn the seat of

[1] This translation of the Panchen Lama's letter has been taken from Turner's (pp. ix-xii), with a few suggestions from Markham's (pp. 1-3), notably the two sets of parentheses which help to clarify passages which otherwise might sound confusing. Markham does not cite a separate source for his rendering, so it must have been taken from Turner's also, with the slight changes in wording he has noted. Most of the latter do not appear to clarify the subject in any way, so we have ignored them. In the case of one or two awkward-sounding sentences, we have altered the order of the phrases to make the meaning clear.

[2] It must be remembered that this letter was transmitted in Persian, the diplomatic language of the Moghul Court in India, wherein such expressions as these were simple acts of courtesy. The Panchen Lama was not necessarily referring either to the God of the Christians or to his own supreme deity. Markham evades the issue by merely printing "Praise that . . . ," omitting the word between.

157

justice and power, that mankind may enjoy the blessings of peace and affluence under the shadow of your bosom.

By your favor, I am the Rajah and Lama of this country, and rule over a number of subjects, a circumstance with which you have no doubt been acquainted by travelers from these parts. I have been repeatedly informed that you have engaged in hostilities against the Deb Judhur [Rajah of Bhutan], to which, it is said, the Deb's own criminal conduct has given rise, in committing ravages and other outrages on your frontiers. As he is of a rude and ignorant race (past times are not destitute of instances of the like faults, which his avarice tempted him to commit), it is not unlikely that he has now renewed those instances; and the ravages and plunder which he may have committed on the outskirts of the Bengal and Behar provinces have given you provocation to send your avenging army against him.

Nevertheless, his party has been defeated, many of his people have been killed, three forts have been taken from him, and he has met with the punishment he deserved. And it is as evident as the sun [that] your army has been victorious, and that, if you had been desirous of it, you might have entirely extirpated him in the space of two days, for he had not the power to resist your efforts. But I now take [it] upon me to be his mediator, and to represent to you that, as the said Deb Rajah is dependent upon the Dalai Lama who rules in this country with unlimited sway (though on account of his being in his minority, the charge of the government and administration for the present is committed to me), should you persist in offering further molestation to the Deb's country, it will irritate both the [Dalai] Lama and all his subjects against you. Therefore, from a regard to our religion and customs, I request [that] you will cease from all hostilities against him, and in doing this you will confer the greatest favor and friendship upon me.

I have reprimanded the Deb [Rajah] for his past conduct, and I have admonished him to desist from his evil practices in future, and to be submissive to you in all things. I am persuaded that he will conform to the advice which I have given him, and it will be necessary that you treat him with compassion and clemency. As to my part, I am but a holy man, and it is the custom of my sect, with the rosary in our hands, to pray for the welfare of all mankind and for the peace and happiness of the inhabitants of this country. And I do now, with my head uncovered, entreat that you may cease all hostilities against the Deb [Rajah] in future.

It would be needless to add to the length of this letter, as the bearer of it, who is a gosain, will represent to you all particulars, and it is hoped that you will comply therewith. In this country the worship of the Almighty is the profession of all.[3] We poor creatures are in nothing equal to you. Having a few things in hand, I send them to you as tokens of remembrance, and hope for your acceptance of them.

[3] Here the Persian letter writer probably altered a reference to the Buddha.

ᐯᐯᐯᐯᐯᐯᐯᐯᐯᐯ

A P P E N D I X   C

ᐯᐯᐯᐯᐯᐯᐯᐯᐯᐯ

THE PRINCIPAL ARTICLES OF THE
TREATY OF PEACE WITH BHUTAN
IN 1774[1]

1. That the Honorable Company, wholly from consideration for the distress to which the Bhootans represented themselves to be reduced, and from the desire of living in peace with their neighbours, will relinquish all the lands which belonged to the Deb Rajah before the commencement of the war with the Rajah of Cooch Behar, namely to the eastward, the lands of Chitchacotta and Pangola-haut, and to the westward, the lands of Kyruntee, Marragaut and Luckypoor.

2. That for the possession of the Chitchacotta Province, the Deb Rajah shall pay an annual tribute of five Tangun horses to the Honorable Company which was the acknowledgement paid to the Behar Rajah.[2]

3. That the Deb Rajah shall deliver up Dhujinder Narain, Rajah of Cooch Behar, together with his brother the Dewan Deo, who is confined with him.

4. That the Bhootans, being merchants, shall have the same privilege of trade as formerly, without the payment of duties, and their caravan shall be allowed to go to Rungpoor (Rangpur) annually.

---

[1] Aitchison, xiv, 81-82.

[2] Note that this is a fairly tacit announcement of the change of suzerainty in Cooch Behar. Incidentally, the Tangun horses were well described by Turner (pp. 21-23), although his explanation of the name on p. 22 is probably inaccurate; see Hobson-Jobson, p. 898.

5. That the Deb Rajah shall never cause incursions to be made into the country [of Cooch Behar], nor in any respect whatever molest the ryots [tenant farmers] that have come under the Honorable Company's subjection.[3]

Signed and ratified at Fort William, April 25, 1774.

[3] Articles 6-10 are omitted here since they are irrelevant for our purposes.

A P P E N D I X   D

SUMMARY OF TURNER'S LIST OF ARTICLES
IN THE TIBETAN TRADE IN 1782

TURNER stated in the list appended to his report on Tibetan trade for Warren Hastings that Tibet exported to China gold dust, diamonds, pearls and coral, a small quantity of musk,[1] Tibetan woolen cloth,[2] lambskins and otter pelts from Bengal. While China sent to Tibet gold and silver brocades, plain silks, satins, black teas of four or five different types, tobacco, silver bullion, cinnabar and quicksilver, some chinaware,[3] trumpets, cymbals, and other musical instruments,[4] furs such as sable, ermine, and black fox, and dried fruits of various kinds.[5]

Tibet sent to Nepal rock salt, borax, and gold dust, and received in return coinage (not since some twenty years before Turner's visit, however), coarse cloth including

[1] China was not totally dependent on Tibet for musk, because the musk deer also live in South and West China.

[2] Forrest, III, p. 1077, has added the word "twilled," in his reproduction of Turner's original report preserved in the Foreign Dept. of the Govt. of India. This is quite in order, as most of the Tibetan fabrics are made with a twill weave.

[3] Because of the dangers of breakage on the long journey from China to Tibet, porcelain cups are highly prized in Tibet, and often mounted with silver or gold bases and covers. Examples of mounted cups may be seen at Newark Museum, Newark, New Jersey.

[4] Among the more popular Chinese instruments used by Tibetans are conical oboes. The writer has seen small metal hand-trumpets, and long copper horns (up to 12 feet in length), being made in Chengtu, Szechuan, for the Tibetan trade.

[5] Turner, p. 381. Some of these preserved fruits were apparently sent on to Bhutan, because Turner speaks of being served "some preserved fruits of China and Cashmeer," when visiting the Deb Rajah (*ibid.*, p. 71).

guzzy,[6] rice and copper.[7] Meanwhile, he said that Nepal
was the principal channel through which English commodities and the products of Bengal were carried to Tibet,
though at the time of writing commerce was still very
limited, not yet having recovered from the effects of the
Gurkha conquest.[8] The English articles imported by the
Tibetans included broadcloth, of which the colors most in
demand were yellow and red (the colors worn by the
lamas), and trinkets such as snuff boxes, smelling bottles,
knives, scissors, and telescopes.[9] Of spices, the Tibetans
especially wanted cloves, as they were the principal in-
gredients in the incense sticks which were kept constantly
burning before men of high rank. (Tibetan cooking,
Turner explained, did not make use of spices.) The Tibetans also imported from Bengal nutmegs, sandalwood,
pearls,[10] emeralds, sapphires, lapis lazuli, coral, jet and
amber, conch shells, heavy gold brocades—especially those
from Gujerat in Western India, Malta cloth, guzzy, to-

6 Guzzy was the Anglo-Indian term for a very poor kind of cotton
cloth. See Col. Henry Yule and A. C. Burnell, *Hobson-Jobson*, a Glossary
of Anglo-Indian Words and Phrases (London, 1886), p. 309.

7 Turner, p. 382. Although, as we have seen above, Tibet had her own
copper mines, their output was no doubt limited, due to the strong prejudice against mining; and a great deal of copper was needed for making
images, the casting of which was considered an act of merit.

8 Turner (p. 370) says that the profits from the limited commerce at
the time of his visit were enjoyed by a few opulent gosains, and by an
agent living at Tashilhunpo who was acting jointly for a Kashmiri
merchant named Mull, and Gopal Das (a Bengali name).

9 Turner (p. 382) calls them "optic glasses"; but his report in the
Foreign Office of the Government of India says "spying glasses" (Forrest,
Selections, iii, p. 1078).

10 The other list (Forrest, *ibid.*) mentions "diamonds," between the
sandalwood and the pearls. These are probably the same diamonds that
were mentioned above as being sent to China. Diamonds have never been
prized as jewelry in either Tibet or China (until this century), because
of a strong prejudice against faceted stones, as opposed to those cut *en
cabochon*—to which the diamond does not lend itself, being colorless and
rather uninteresting without facets. In China diamonds were used for
drills, and the diamond dust as abrasive, in cutting other stones, such
as jades.

bacco, indigo and otter skins.[11] They paid for these with gold dust, musk and borax.[12]

From Bhutan, according to Turner, the Tibetans imported more English broadcloth (brought from Bengal), Rangpur leather, tobacco, coarse cotton cloth including guzzy, paper, rice, sandalwood, indigo and madder. In return, the Bhutanese obtained gold dust, tea (from China), Tibetan woolen cloth, and salt.[13]

Ladakh, on the border of West Tibet, was the mart for trade between Kashmir and Tashilhunpo, and in return for the wool of the shawl goat which the Tibetans brought there for the Kashmiri traders,[14] they obtained finished shawls, dried fruits such as apricots, raisins and kismishes (small seedless raisins), currants and dates, as well as almonds and saffron.[15]

Lastly, Turner said that the Kalmuks brought to Tashilhunpo horses, camels,[16] and Russian leather.[17] Elsewhere, he had said that a large party of these people had come to Tashilhunpo while he was there, bringing horses, furs, Russian leather and skins full of butter, as religious tribute, in the form of offerings to the Panchen Lama.[18]

[11] Turner, pp. 382-83.   [12] *Ibid.*, p. 382.   [13] *Ibid.*, p. 383.

[14] For references to the shawl goat see *ibid.*, pp. 356, 371.

[15] *Ibid.*, p. 384. The saffron was used as a yellow dye for the hats and shawls of the *Gelugpa* lamas. In his book (*ibid.*) Turner lists another yellow dye, gamboge, but this commodity is not mentioned in the original list (Forrest, *Selections*, p. 1074), and it certainly was not a product of Northwest India, though it might have been imported to Tibet by Kashmiri merchants via Nepal or Bhutan.

[16] Turner uses the term "dromedaries," but this has now come to be used almost exclusively for the one-humped Near Eastern camels, and the Kalmuks and other Mongols use the two-humped Bactrian variety almost exclusively.

[17] *Ibid.*, p. 384. In his list, this entry appears as "Khumbauk to Tibet." On p. 273, he defines Khumbâk (note difference in spelling) as a tribe of Kalmuks. See next note.

[18] *Ibid.*, pp. 273-74. Turner said that the people came from a place situated on the river "Sullum," fifty-two days' journey away, by way of Lhasa and "Daum." We have been unable to find any logical equivalents for "Sullum" and "Daum," unless perhaps the former refers to the Selenga River in the northern part of Outer Mongolia, and the latter to Tomsk; but one would not ordinarily pass through Tomsk on the way from Lhasa to a point on the Selenga.

⋀⋀⋀⋀⋀⋀⋀⋀⋀

BIBLIOGRAPHY

⋁⋁⋁⋁⋁⋁⋁⋁⋁

THE PRINCIPAL WORKS CITED[1]

I Occidental Sources

Aitchison, C. U. (compiler), *A Collection of Treaties, Engagements and Sanads*, Relating to India and Neighboring Countries (Calcutta, 1929, 1930, 1931). Vol. xiv contains the treaties etc. relating to Tibet, Nepal and Bhutan.
Each section of this work contains a brief historical survey of the region discussed. These are useful, but not very reliable for reference, and should be checked.

Amiot, Fr., *Memoires concernant l'histoire, les sciences, les arts, les mœurs, les usages des chinois par les missionaires de Pé-kin* (Paris, 1783). Vol. ix contains contemporary material regarding the visit of the Sixth Panchen Lama to Peking.

Aspinall, A., *Cornwallis in Bengal*, The Administrative and Judicial Reforms of Lord Cornwallis in Bengal, Together with Accounts of the Commercial Expansion of the East India Company 1786-1793, etc., *University of Manchester Historical Series*, no. lx (Manchester, 1931). Contains brief references to eighteenth century Tibet and Nepal.

Astley, Thomas (editor), *A New General Collection of Voyages and Travels* (London, 1747).
Commonly known as "Astley's Voyages," this contains a section on the early European travelers to Tibet.

---

[1] This list of books represents only the works that have a more or less direct bearing on the early history of Tibet and the English relations with Tibet in the eighteenth century. It does not include a number of other books and articles cited in the notes to support minor points and digressions.

Barrow, John, *Some Account of the Public Life and a Selection from the Unpublished Writings of the Earl of Macartney* (London, 1807), two vols.
Vol. II mentions the supposed effects of the Chinese campaign against Nepal on Anglo-Chinese relations.

Bell, Sir Charles A., *Tibet, Past and Present* (Oxford, 1924).
Extensive historical survey of Tibetan history and politics from the official British point of view.

——, *The People of Tibet* (Oxford, 1928).
An excellent study of Tibetan life and customs.

——, *The Religion of Tibet* (Oxford, 1931).
A rather rambling discussion of Lamaism, with quotations from Tibetan texts; unfortunately this omits many important aspects of the religion, emphasizing the literary approach.

——, *Portrait of the Dalai Lama* (London, 1946).
A recapitulation of his previous books with considerable new material on Tibetan history and politics in recent times.

Bushell, S. W., "The Early History of Tibet from Chinese Sources," *Journal of the Royal Asiatic Society,* XII (London, 1880).
This presents in translation the passages relating to Tibet in the T'ang histories.

Bysack, Gaur Das, "Notes on a Buddhist Monastery at Bhot Bagan (Howrah)," *Journal of the Asiatic Society of Bengal,* LIX, 1890 (Calcutta, 1891).
Contains a vast amount of original material from Indian sources on Purangir, his life and his times.

Callaey, Frédégand, "Missionaires capucins et la civilisation thibétaine" *Études Françiscaines,* XLVI (1934).
Some testimony on the achievements of the Capuchin Mission in Tibet in the early eighteenth century.

Cambridge History of India (Cambridge, 1932).
Only the briefest references to Tibet until recent times.

Castéra, J. H. (translator), *Ambassade au Thibet et au Boutan* (Paris, 1800), two vols.
The French translation of Turner's book with some additional notes.

Chapman, F. Spencer, *Lhasa, the Holy City* (London, 1938), An excellent description of modern Tibet and its politics, with many references to past factors that have influenced it.

Cordier, Henri, *Bibliotheca Sinica*, iv (Paris, 1907-1908), Supplement, iv (Paris, 1924).
Useful bibliographical references to many aspects of Tibetan studies.

Dalrymple, Alexander, *Oriental Repository* (London, 1808; previously published in periodical form, in the eighteenth century).
This contained the first appearance in English of several important documents concerning Tibet which were later republished by Turner.

D'Anville, Jean Baptiste Bourgignon, *Nouvel atlas de la Chine, de la Tartarie-chinoise et du Thibet* (The Hague, 1737).
Contains interesting early maps of Tibet and adjacent regions.

Das, Sarat Chandra, *Tibetan-English Dictionary* (Calcutta, 1902).
Still the best general dictionary of the Tibetan language. The very full definitions render it an encyclopedia on Tibetan life and the Lamaist religion.

———, "Contributions on the Religion, History &c. of Tibet," *Journal of the Asiatic Society of Bengal*, l (Calcutta, 1881), li (1882).
While much of this material is valuable as having been drawn from Tibetan sources, these essays are full of questionable inferences and minor inaccuracies.

———, "Tibet a Dependency of Mongolia (1643-1716)," "Tibet under her last Kings (1434-1642)," "A Short History of

the House of Phagdu," *Journal of the Asiatic Society of Bengal,* new series I (Calcutta, 1905).
The remarks about the last reference apply also to these articles.

Das, Taraknath, *British Expansion in Tibet* (Calcutta, 1929).
A fanatically anti-British writer presents his personal views on the subject, perpetuating some past errors and introducing new ones.

Davies, A. Mervyn, *Warren Hastings, Maker of British India* (London, 1935).
A well-written biography, but it devotes little space to Hastings' Tibetan interests.

Desideri, Ippolito, *An Account of Tibet,* the Travels of Ippolito Desideri of Pistoia, edited by Filippo de Filippi, introduction by C. J. Wessels (revised edition, London, 1937).
A valuable book of personal experiences in eighteenth century Tibet, very well edited.

Dictionary of National Biography (London, 1885-1901).
This contains the biographies of Hastings, Bogle, Turner, Cornwallis, Macartney, and other persons who figure in the present study.

Diskalkar, D. B., "Bogle's Embassy to Tibet," *The Indian Historical Quarterly,* IX (Calcutta, 1933).
The author has based some questionable conclusions on "unpublished documents," several of which had previously appeared.

———, "Tibeto-Nepalese War, 1788-1793," *Journal of the Bihar and Orissa Research Society,* XIX (Patna, 1933).
This contains valuable documents on the Gurkha War, many of which are not otherwise available. But the remarks about his previous article are equally applicable.

Du Halde, J. B., *History of China* (London, 1736). The English translation of his *Description geographique, historique, chronologique, politique et physique de l'empire de la Chine et de la Tartarie Chinoise* (Paris, 1735).

The section on Tibet contains little of any importance, but is interesting as having been one of the sources of Hastings' early knowledge of Tibet, before Bogle brought back more detailed information.

Eden, The Honorable Ashley, et al., *Political Missions to Bootan* (Calcutta, 1865).
A valuable collection of documents relating to British relations with Tibet's neighbor, Bhutan.

Fairbank, J. K., and S. Y. Têng, "On the Ch'ing Tributary System," *Harvard Journal of Asiatic Studies*, vi (1941).
A careful analysis of the method by which the Chinese Empire conducted trade with her dependencies and other foreign countries, including Nepal and Tibet.

Forrest, Sir George W., *The Administration of Warren Hastings 1772-1785*, reviewed and illustrated from original documents (Calcutta, 1892).
Contains very little about Hastings' aspirations regarding Tibet.

————, *Selections from the Letters, Despatches, and Other State Papers Preserved in the Foreign Department of the Government of India 1772-1785* (Calcutta, 1890), three vols.
Contains documents of the Bogle and Turner missions.

Francke, Reverend A. H., "The Kingdom of gNya-khri-btsanpo, the First King of Tibet," *Journal and Proceedings of the Asiatic Society of Bengal*, vi (Calcutta, 1910).
Produces new evidence for the origins of Tibetan culture, at variance with the traditional early history of Tibet.

Gleig, Reverend G. R., *Memoirs of the Life of the Right Hon. Warren Hastings* (London, 1841), three vols.
The most complete biography of Hastings, containing original letters and despatches.

Gundry, R. S., *China and her Neighbours*, France in Indo-China, Russia and China, India and Tibet (London, 1893).
A semi-popular presentation, containing a brief sketch of Anglo-Tibetan relations.

Hodgson, B. H., "On the Commerce of Nepal," *Selections from the Records of the Government of Bengal*, no. xxvii (Calcutta, 1857), reprinted in *Essays on the Languages, Literature and Religion of Nepal and Tibet* (London, 1874).
Useful for comparison with earlier lists by Bogle, Turner and Kirkpatrick.

Holdich, Colonel Sir Thomas, *Tibet, the Mysterious* (New York, 1906).
Mostly an account of Tibetan exploration, based to a considerable degree on Sandberg's *Exploration of Tibet*, perpetuating many of the latter's serious errors.

Hummel, Arthur W. (editor), *Eminent Chinese of the Ch'ing Period* (Washington, D. C., 1943, 1944); two vols.
Much useful material on China's contacts with Tibet is contained in the biographies of the Chinese and Manchu officials involved.

Huth, Georg, *Geschichte des Buddhismus in der Mongolei*, from the Tibetan of Jigs-med nam-mka (Strassburg, 1892, 1896); two vols.
A pedantically edited translation of a Tibetan history of Mongolian Lamaism, with numerous mistakes in the rendering of dates, titles, Chinese terms, etc.

Ikbal Ali Shah, The Sirdar, *Nepal: the Home of the Gods* (London, 1938).
A rather popular history, strongly sympathetic toward the Nepalese.

Imbault-Huart, C. C., "Histoire de la conquête du Népâl par les Chinois sous la règne de Tc'ie Long (1792)," *Journal Asiatique*, 7th series, xii (Paris, 1878).
A translation of the first account of the Nepal campaign from the *Shêng wu chi*. The translation is reasonably accurate, but the notes are often misleading.

———, "Un Épisode des relations diplomatiques de la Chine avec le Népâl en 1842," *Revue de l'Extrême Orient*, iii (Paris, 1887).

Contains interesting comments on the Sino-Nepalese tributary relationship in general.

Kaye, John William, *Lives of Indian Officers*, Illustrative of the History of the Civil and Military Service of India (London, 1873).
Contains the biography of Lord Cornwallis.

Kirkpatrick, Colonel (William), *An Account of the Kingdom of Nepaul* (London, 1811).
An important source for the study of eighteenth century Nepal, and its relations with India, the East India Company, and Tibet.

Koeppen, Carl Friedrich, *Die Religion des Buddha* (Berlin, 1857, 1859); two vols.
Vol. ii, "Die Lamaische Hierarchie und Kirche," is a detailed study of Lama Buddhism with its historical and political aspects. Although much evidence has since been accumulated, this still remains an important sourcebook.

Landon, Perceval, *Nepal* (London, 1928); two vols.
A very well written, comprehensive history of Nepal, with full discussions of Nepalese geography, history, and politics.

————, *The Opening of Tibet*, an Account of Lhasa and the Country and People of Central Tibet, etc. (New York, 1905).
A popular book, containing in its first chapter, on former explorations, brief references to Bogle and Turner.

Lee, Wei-kuo, *Tibet in Modern World Politics (1774-1922)* (New York, 1931).
Unsatisfactory in its scholarship, this is especially weak in dealing with the early period of Anglo-Tibetan relations, and makes unwarranted generalizations about Sino-Tibetan politics.

Lévi, Sylvain, *"Le Népal,* étude historique d'un royaume Hindou," *Annales du Musée Guimet,* xvii (1905), xviii (1905), xix (1908).
An even more scholarly study of Nepal than that of

Landon, and one from which the latter apparently drew heavily.

Ludwig, Ernest, *The Visit of the Teshoo Lama to Peking* (Peking, 1904).
Consists principally of translations of memorial tablets inscribed by the Ch'ien-lung Emperor to commemorate this event. The notes and additional material are often open to question.

Markham, Clements, *Narratives of the Mission of George Bogle to Tibet and of the Journey of Thomas Manning to Lhasa* (London, 1876). (We have used the second edition of 1879, in preparing this study.)
This is the primary source for the story of Bogle's Mission; while the long introduction contains a wealth of material on Tibetan exploration in general, up to the time of writing. The explanatory notes, however, must be carefully checked for accuracy.

Parker, E. H., "Manchu Relations with Tibet, or Si-tsang," *Journal of the China Branch of the Royal Asiatic Society,* new series, XXI, 1886 (Shanghai, 1887).
The writer's carelessness is apparent in the translations from Chinese sources.

Petech, L., "The Missions of Bogle and Turner According to the Tibetan Texts," *T'oung Pao,* XXXIX (1949).
Brief but valuable information, well presented.

Pritchard, Earl H., "The Crucial Years of Early Anglo-Chinese Relations 1750-1800," *Research Studies of the State College of Washington,* IV, 1936 (Pullman, Washington, 1937).
Contains material on the Macartney Mission, and the sequels to the Chinese campaign against Nepal.

Robbins, Helen H., *Our First Ambassador to China,* an Account of the Life of George, Earl of Macartney (London, 1908).
A full biography of Lord Macartney.

Rockhill, W. W., *The Dalai Lamas of Lhasa and their Relations with the Manchu Emperors of China 1644-1908* (Leyden,

1910), (originally appeared in *T'oung-pao*, series 2, XI, 1910).

Since it was derived from primary Chinese sources, this is generally quoted as the authoritative work on the history of Sino-Tibetan relations, though it has many errors in dates, citations, and minor statements of fact. However, the generalizations and conclusions are for the most part very sound, having been drawn from the author's long acquaintance with the subject.

————, *The Life of the Buddha* (London, 1884).
This includes a brief treatment of the early history of Tibet.

————, "Notes on the Ethnology of Tibet," Based on the Collections in the United States National Museum, *Annual Report of the Smithsonian Institution for the year ending June 30, 1893*, Report of the U. S. National Museum (Washington, 1895).
A valuable study, based on the author's personal experiences while exploring Northeastern Tibet.

————, "Tibet, A Geographical, Ethnographical, and Historical Sketch Derived from Chinese Sources," *Journal of the Royal Asiatic Society of Great Britain and Ireland*, 1891 (no vol. number), republished in book form, Peking, 1939.
This contains much useful information, but all statements should be carefully checked for accuracy.

Ronaldshay, Earl of, *Lands of the Thunderbolt*, Sikhim, Chumbi and Bhutan (London and Bombay, 1923).
A well-written popular account of the Tibetan borderlands of India, and their history.

Ross, Charles, *Correspondence of Charles, First Marquis Cornwallis* (London, 1859), three vols.
Many documents are presented relating to Cornwallis' administration of Bengal, but comparatively few of these deal with the problems of Nepal and Tibet.

Rouire, Dr. (A.M.F.), *La rivalité Anglo-Russe au XIXe siècle en Asie* (Paris, 1908).

A strongly biased anti-British work, with comparatively little on the eighteenth century relations between Bengal and Tibet.

Sandberg, Graham, *The Exploration of Tibet*, its History and Particulars from 1623 to 1904 (Calcutta, 1904).
Apparently a quickly written journalistic project to take advantage of popular interest in Tibet at the time of the Younghusband Expedition to Lhasa. Though often quoted, it is full of misstatements and inaccuracies.

Sarcar, S. C., "Some Notes on the Intercourse of Bengal with the Northern Countries in the Second Half of the Eighteenth Century," *Bengal Past and Present*, XLI (Calcutta, 1931). A detailed account from records of the East India Company preserved in Calcutta, presented with careful scholarship.

Sarkar, S. C., "A note on Puran Gir Gosain," *Bengal Past and Present*, XLIII (Calcutta, 1932).
In spite of the difference in spelling the writer's name, this was written by the author of the preceding article, and is characterized by the same careful scholarship. However, it contains little that was not previously presented by Bysack and others.

Schlagintweit, Emil, *Buddhism in Tibet* (Leipzig and London, 1863).
An important book on Lamaism, though it has been somewhat outdated by the writings of Waddell, Bell, and others.

Staël-Holstein, Baron A. von, "Notes on Two Lama Paintings," *Journal of the American Oriental Society*, LII (1932).
Useful biographical notes on the antecedents, real and legendary, of the earlier Dalai and Panchen Lamas, written with most careful scholarship.

———, "Remarks on an Eighteenth Century Lamaist Document," *Kuo-hsüeh chi-k'an*, I (Peking, 1923).
Notes on the first Grand Lamas of Peking, including the

Sanskya Hutukhtu who was a friend of the Sixth Panchen Lama.

Staunton, Sir George, Bart., *An Authentic Account of an Embassy from the King of Great Britain to the Emperor of China* (London, 1797); two vols.
The official account of the Macartney Mission, with references to the recent Chinese campaign against Nepal.

Turner, Captain Samuel, *An Account of an Embassy to the Court of the Teshoo Lama in Tibet* (London, 1800; second ed., 1806).
The primary source for the Turner Mission, with other documents relating to Tibet, in the appendices.

Waddell, L. A., *The Buddhism of Tibet, or Lamaism* (London, 1899; second ed., Cambridge, 1939).
Though the writer's approach is not particularly sympathetic toward the Tibetans, this has long been considered the best book on Lamaism in general. Both the illustrations and large sections of the text have been taken from previous works on the subject.

————, *Lhasa and its Mysteries*, with a Record of the Expedition of 1903-1904 (London, 1905).
Contains brief references to earlier Tibetan history, and interesting remarks on Tibetan life and religion, told in a semi-popular vein.

Walsh, E. H. C., "The Coinage of Tibet," *Memoirs of the Asiatic Society of Bengal*, ii (Calcutta, 1907).
Unfortunately this contains numerous errors which diminish its value for reference.

Wessels, C., S.J., *Early Jesuit Travellers in Central Asia, 1603-1721* (The Hague, 1924).
This mentions early travelers to Tibet.

White, John Claude, *Sikhim and Bhutan* (London, 1909).
A rather popular account of these two countries and their

relations with the English, enlivened by personal reminiscences of the Tibetan borderlands of India.

Wilson, H. H., *A Glossary of Judicial and Revenue Terms of British India*, edited by A. C. Ganguli and N. D. Basu (Calcutta, 1940).
This is indispensable for the meanings of technical terms, either ignored or inadequately discussed by the authors of *Hobson-Jobson*.

Wright, Daniel (editor), *History of Nepal*, translated from the *Parbatiya* by Munshi Shew Shunker Singh and Pandit Shri Gunanand (Cambridge, 1877).
Contains an exceedingly biased Gurkha account of the Sino-Nepalese campaign of 1792.

Younghusband, Sir Francis, *India and Tibet*, a History of the Relations which have Subsisted Between the two Countries from the time of Warren Hastings to 1910; with a Particular Account of the Mission to Lhasa of 1904 (London, 1910).
A semi-popular book, apparently written in self-justification, it contains nothing of special significance for the eighteenth century period.

Yule, Colonel Henry (editor), *The Book of Ser Marco Polo* (London, 1871); two vols.
The editor's very full notes contain some interesting observations on Tibet of the Middle Ages, and relations between the Mongols and Tibetans.

————, and A. C. Burnell, *Hobson-Jobson*: Being a Glossary of Anglo-Indian Colloquial Words and Phrases, and of Kindred Terms, etc., (London, 1886).
A very useful reference book for unfamiliar terms used by the Anglo-Indian writers from Bogle and Turner down to recent times.

(Anonymous), "The Buddhist Monastery at Ghoosery," *Bengal: Past and Present*, xxvi (1923).
Brief notes on Purangir and the monastery he founded.

II Chinese Sources[2]

Chin-shih chung-hsi shih-jih tui-chao piao, compiled by Chêng Hao-shêng (1936).

A table of dates in the Chinese calendar from 1516 to 1941, with their Occidental equivalents; indispensable for Western students working with Chinese historical records.

Ch'ing li-ch'ao shih-lu, "The Veritable Records of the Ch'ing Dynasty" (Tokyo, 1937).

These are the authentic Court records of the Ch'ing Dynasty (1644-1911), comprising imperial edicts, memorials, and descriptions of special events, written on the spot by a corps of official recorders; with accurate dates and full presentations. At the end of each reign, the material for that period was compiled, and therefore the section of the *Shih-lu* for a given reign bears the name of the emperor who was then ruling. Thus the Ch'ien-lung section, from which we have most frequently quoted, carries the full title of *Kao-tsung Shun-huang-ti shih-lu.*

Ch'ing-shih kao, "The Draft History of the Ch'ing Dynasty," compiled by Chao Erh-sun and others (1928).

The history of the Manchu Dynasty compiled under the new Chinese Republic, but never officially approved because some of the revolutionaries considered it pro-dynastic. On the whole, this is generally considered to be a very fair and balanced compilation of past records, though a certain carelessness is apparent in the handling of names and dates.

Ch'ing-shih lieh-chüan, "Various Biographies from the Ch'ing History" (1928).

Lives of famous men of the Manchu Dynasty, including the generals who served in the Tibetan campaigns.

Chiu T'ang-shu, "The Old History of the T'ang Dynasty," compiled by Liu Hsü and others, in the 10th century A.D.

[2] The type of Chinese book listed here is characteristically a compilation rather than an original work, so the name of the author (or authors) was considered rather unimportant, and in many cases does not appear at all. For this reason we have listed them alphabetically by titles.

This is especially interesting for its section devoted to other countries and peoples with whom China had relations in the early Middle Ages, including the Tibetans.

Hsi-tsang pei-wên, "Tibetan Tablet Inscriptions," compiled by Mêng-pao (1851).

A collection of the Chinese inscriptions on the memorial tablets in Lhasa, commemorating the principal events in Sino-Tibetan relations, including the various Manchu military expeditions, assembled by a Manchu Amban at Lhasa.

Hsi-tsang t'u-k'ao, "Investigation of Tibetan Maps" (1886).

An important study of Tibetan geography, reissued several times during the Ch'ing Dynasty.

Hsü Tsang-shih chien, "The Revised History of Tibet," translated from Tibetan into Chinese by Liu Li-ch'ien (Chengtu, 1947).

A good example of the native Tibetan histories, a tedious compendium of long names and titles, with little vital information.

(Chin-ting) Kuo-erh-k'o chi-lüeh, "The Official Digest of the Records of the Gurkha Campaign" (compiled in 1795).

A very rare book containing the official documents of the campaign of 1791-1792 in Tibet and Nepal.

Shêng wu chi, "Chronicles of the Imperial Military Exploits," compiled by Wei Yüan (1846).

Detailed accounts of the chief campaigns by which the Manchu Emperors extended their empire; carefully compiled by an eminent Chinese scholar who had accurate records at his disposal.

Ta-Ch'ing hui-tien, "Collected Statutes of the Ch'ing Dynasty" (K'ang-hsi edition of 1690, Kuang-hsü edition of 1900).

This work contains the basic laws and regulations for the management of the Manchu Court and the governing of the Chinese Empire. It was issued five times during the dynasty, but only the first and last editions have been directly used in writing this book.

Ta-Ch'ing hui-tien shih-li, "Supplement to the Collected Statutes of the Ch'ing Dynasty" (Kuang-hsü edition of 1900).

This supplement to the last two editions of the preceding work contains the dynastic laws and regulations with additional commentaries, dated instances of the breaking of laws or reinforcement of them, and very detailed statistics on many subjects concerned with the Manchu government of China.

Ta-Ch'ing i-t'ung chih, "Gazeteer of the Whole Ch'ing Realm," compiled by Chiang Ting-hsi and others (revised edition of 1849).

An account of all the territories ruled by the Manchu Dynasty at the height of its power; with geographical and historical data on each area, including Tibet.

Tung-hua lu, "Records of China," compiled by Wang Hsien-ch'ien and others, (1887).

Like the *Shih-lu,* this contains edicts, memorials, and descriptions of Court events; but they are presented in a somewhat more abbreviated and more accessible form. (The earlier sections were drastically censored by the Ch'ien-lung Emperor who was seeking to "purify" the memory of his ancestors; but those for his own reign and those of his successors are quite complete.)

Wei-Tsang t'u-shih, "Maps and Information Concerning Eastern and Western Tibet," by Ma Chieh (1792).

A geographical, ethnographical, historical, and administrative account of Tibet, published on the occasion of the completion of Manchu Imperial control over Tibet.

INDEX

Abdul Kadir Khan, 75-77, 113 n. 52, 125, 127, 128, 130.
Acharya, 141 n. 75.
Agnew, Alexander, 119.
A-kuei, General, 123.
Altan Khan of the Tumets, 10.
Ambans, 17, 40, 45 n. 73, 46, 87, (104), 113, 115, 121-22, 128, 133, 141, 150.
amber, 59, 60, 63, 163.
American Revolution, 83, 106.
Amiot, Fr. J.J.M., 70, 78 n. 94.
Andrade, Fr. Antonio, 18-19, 21 n. 77.
architecture, Tibetan, 7-8, 11.
Assam, 25, 36, 39-40, 62, 147.
Astley's Voyages, 21 n. 77, 35.
Atisha, 9, 10.
atsara lamas, 141 n. 75.

Bahadur Sahi, Regent of Nepal, 130.
Bell, Sir Charles A., 22 n. 80, 55-56.
Bell, John, *Travels*, 35.
Benares, 24, 29, 61, 124.
Bengal, 9, 22, 24, 25-26, 27, 28, 29, 32, 34, 40, 46-51, 52-54, 58, 61, 63-64, 66-67, 74, 76, 87, 91, 93, 94, 95, 97-100, 104, 107, 119, 137, 142, 143, 144-45, 147, 148, 156, 158, 162, 163; Government of, (25), (28), 103, 105-6, 139.
Bengal Infantry, 130.
Bhatgaon, 108-9.
Bhutan, 3, 16, 19, 22, 24, 25-26, 27-29, 35-41, 44-45, 46, 47, 48, 51, 52-53, 56, 62, 67, 74 n. 88, 80, 84, 85, 91-92, 95-96, 99, 109, 127, 132, 142, 146, 149-50, 151, 155, 158, 160-61, 164.
Bodh Gaya, 24, 49.

Bogle, George, viii, 31-53, 54-65, 66, 67-69, 74, 80-81, 82, 84-85, 89 n. 29, 92, 94, 96, 97, 109-10, 132 n. 46, 141 n. 75, 142, 145-46, 150.
Boglepur, 81 n. 102.
Bön religion, 7, 8.
Bootan, *see* Bhutan.
borax, 21, 41 n. 52, 56-57, 97, 99, 162, 164.
Boutan, *see* Bhutan.
Brahmaputra River, 39.
British goods, (24), 32, 83, 104-5, 118, 136-37, 163, 164.
broadcloth, 58, 60, 63-64, 163-64.
Brunnert, H. S., 112 n. 51.
Buddhism, Indian 6, 8-9, 56; Tibetan, *see* Lamaism.
Buriat Mongols, 60.

Cabral, Fr. John, 19.
Cacella, Fr. Stephen, 19.
Calcutta, 26, 30, 35, 46, 49, 64, 66-67, 76, 80-81, 82, 84, 102, 114, 126, 128, 139-41.
calendar, Tibetan, 7, 79 n. 99.
Calmucks, *see* Kalmuks.
camels, 60, 164.
cannon, 124, 126.
Canton, 32 n. 26, 51, 68-69, (122), 138 n. 67, 141.
Capuchins, 19-20, 21 n. 77, 22.
Cashmere, *see* Kashmir.
Castéra, J. H., 77 n. 93, 112 n. 50.
Cathcart, Lieutenant Colonel Charles, 118-19, 137.
Catherine the Great of Russia, 88.
Chait Singh, ruler of Benares, 24, (29).
Chamdo, 133.
Changkya Hutukhtu, Grand Lama of Peking, 49, 71, 74, 113.

181

Ch'êng-tê, 120, (122).
Ch'ien-lung Emperor, *see* Emperors of China.
Chin-ch'uan tribesmen, 123.
China, 3-6, 7, 8 n. 18, 9-10, 12, 13-14, 16, 19, 20, 25, 33, 34, 36, 41, 49, 50-51, 54, 55, 57-58, 61, 80, 84 n. 7, 94, 98, 100, 104, 118-19, 128, 129, 142, 144, 145, 162.
Chinese, 7-8, 13, 15, 18, 45, 57, 58-59, 87-88, 122, 124, 128, 131, 132-34, 137, 139, 140, 142-43, 144.
Ch'ing (Manchu) Dynasty, vii, 12-13, 14-18, 144-50; *see also* Manchus, and Emperors of China.
Chumbi Valley, 132, 150.
Chungpa Hutukhtu, Regent of Tashilhunpo, 73, (79), 82-83, 86-89, 90, 93-95, (99), 103, 105-6, 111-12, 114, 130, 132-33, 141, 146.
Ch'inghai, *see* Kokonor.
cinnabar, 98, 162.
Clavering, Sir John, 64.
cloth, European, 25, 63-64, 90, 163-64; Indian, 58, 63, 163-64; Tibetan, 31, 55, 59, 60, 62, 162-64.
coins and coinage, 34, 62, 99, 108-11, 113, 132, 162.
conches (chanks), 58, 63, 163.
Cooch Behar, 24, 26, 28, 36, 38, 155-56, 160-61.
copper, 98, 163.
coral, 58, 59, 63, 64, 162, 163.
Cornwallis, Lord Charles, 106-7, (114-15), 116-18, 124 n. 18, 125, 126-30, 134-36, 139, 140, (141), 148.
corvée transport, 95.
cotton, 25-26, 163 n. 6, 164.

Daghors, 123.
Dalai Lamas, 10-11; the Third, 10-11; the Fifth, 11, 12-13; the Sixth, 15-16; the Eighth, 23, 24, 25, 46, 47, 50, 70, 73 n. 82, 80, 87, 92-94, 103-4, 115, 121, 128-30, (149), 158.
Daljit Gir, (106), 129, 139-41, (142).
Dalrymple, Alexander, 70 n. 74.

Danchin Banjur, the Kalon, 119, 131, 132.
D'Anville, Jean Baptiste Bourgignon, 20, 29-30.
D'Anville's map of Tibet, 20, 21 n. 77, 29-30, 35 n. 35.
Das, Sarat Chandra, 79.
Das, Taraknath, 89 n. 29.
Davis, Sir John, 84 n. 7.
Davis, Lieutenant Samuel, 83, 84 n. 7, 85.
Deb Rajah of Bhutan, 28-29, 37, 40, 45, 47, 51 notes 91 and 92, 52-53, 84, 91-92, 158-59, 160-61.
Dechenrubje, 42-44, 54.
De Guignes, Joseph, *Histoire générale*, 35.
Della Penna, Fr. R. Orazio, 19 n. 71.
Desheripgay, *see* Dechenrubje.
Desideri, Fr. Ippolito, 16 n. 51, 19-20, 108.
Dinapur, 126.
Diskalkar, 69 n. 71, 113 n. 52.
Dorje Phagmo, 122.
D'Orleans, P. J., 56.
D'Orville, Fr. Albert, 19.
Du Halde, J. B., 20, 21 n. 77, 35.
Duncan, Jonathan, 108 n. 37, 123 n. 14, 124-25, 126-27, 128.
Dundas, Henry, 118-19, 138.
dyes, 32, 62, 63, 164.
Dzungarians, *see* Jungars.

East India Company, The British, vii, 21, 24, 25-26, 27, 28-29, 34, 36, 37-40, 44, 50, 53, 54, 57, 64, 67-68, 75, 82-83, 95-96, 100, 102-3, 107, 117, 118, 128-29, 139, 144-46, 148, 155-56; Court of Directors of, 25, 33 n. 28, 54 n. 2, 66, 102, 118; Select Committee of, 31.
Emperors of China, Manchu, 58, 134, 150; K'ang-hsi Emperor, 14-15, (144); Ch'ien-lung Emperor, 36, 40, 47, (49-50), 67, 67-68 n. 62, 70-80, 86, 90, 92, 112 n. 50, 113, 115-16, 120, 122, 128, 132 n. 45, 134, 135, 143, (144), 149, 150.

England, 25, 34, 84 n. 1, 102, 118-19.
English in India, The, 4, 18, 21, 23-24, 25, 36, 37, 44-45, 47-48, 50-51, 53, 56, 70, 72 n. 80, 75, 79-80, 90 n. 33, 91, 92-94, 105, 114, 115-16, 124, 134, 135 n. 57, 138, 155.
English goods, *see* British goods.

Forrest, G. W., 28 n. 6.
Fort William (Calcutta), 54 n. 2, 141, 161.
France, (64), (70), 83.
Francis, Sir Philip, 64.
Francke, Rev. A. H., 5 n. 6.
fruits, 57, 61, 100, 162, 164.
Fu-k'ang-an, General, 122-23, 124, 126, (128), 129, 130, 131-32, 135, 138, 139, 141, 143.
furs and pelts, 59, 60, 63, 162, 164.

Ganges River, 48-49, 66.
Gelug-pa, see Yellow Cap sect.
Georgi, A. A., *Alphabetum Tibetanum,* 20.
Ghusari, 66, 106, 141, (142).
glassware, 32, 58, 64.
gold, 30-31, 32, (34), 39, 48, 55-56, 58, 59, 60, 61, 63, 97-98, 99, 105 n. 18, 109, 110, 114, 118, 125, 148, 162, 164.
gosain(s), 30, 48, 61-62, 142, 157, 163 n. 8.
Grand Lama of Peking, *see* Changkya Hutukhtu.
Grand Lama of Urga, *see* Jebtsun Dampa Hutukhtu.
Grueber, Fr. John, 19.
Gurkha Conquest of Nepal, 22-24, 56, 108-9, 115, 144.
Gurkha Invasion of Tibet, 113-14, 115-16, 119-20, 121-24, 128, 132 n. 45, 134, 142, 148.
Gurkha Pacification Tablet, 134 n. 56.
Gurkha Rajahs of Nepal: Prithvi Narayan, 23-24, 27, 28 n. 4, 37, 109-10; Pratap Singh Sahi, 51-52; Rana Bahadur Sahi, 115-17, 124-25, 126-27, 128-30, 134, 140 n. 73, 141; Rajendra Vikram Sahi, 111 n. 48, 140 n. 73.

Gurkhas, 22-23, 33 n. 28, 46, (48), 51, 56, 62, 107-114, 119-120, 121, 122-23, 131, 132, 133, 138-39, 143, 150 n. 4.
Gushi Khan, 11, 12 n. 35, 13.
Gyantse, 41, 86 n. 18.
Gyurmed Namgyal, 17, 22.

Hai-lan-ch'a, 123.
Hamilton, Alexander, 31, 35, 43, 84.
Hannibal, 123-24.
Hariharpur, 23 n. 83.
Hastings, Warren, 24, 25, 26, 27-35, 36, 37, 40-41, 42, 43, 45-46, (47), 48, 49-50, 52-53, 54, 64-67, 70-75, 79-80, 82-83, 84, 85, 86, 89, 90-91, 92, 94-95, 100-1, 102-3, 105, 107, 118, 145, 146, 150, 155, 162.
hats, 10, 90.
Hedin, Sven, 78 n. 94.
Herodotus, 55.
Himalayas, 3, 18, 23, 25, 124, 145.
Hindus, 24, 30, 125; *see also* gosains.
Hindustan (India), *see under* India.
Hindustani language, 42.
Ho-shou, 15 n. 49.
Hutukhtu (title), 59, 73 n. 82, 111 n. 49.

India, 4, 6, 7-8, 18, 19-20, 21, 22, 23, 28-29, 33, 51, 55-56, 61, 67, 91, 99, 102, 105, 107, 108, 147, 148.
Indians, 36, 94, 95, 142; *see also* gosains, Hindus, Moghuls, Kashmiris, Mahrattas, Moslems, Pathans.
Indus River, 5, 55.
iron, 57, 62.

Jebtsun Dampa Hutukhtu, Grand Lama of Urga, 49 n. 86, 88.
Jehol, 69, 70, 78, 138.
Jesuits, 19, 70.
Jones, Captain, 27.
Jongka (Dzongka), 114-19.
Jungars, 15-16, 17-18, 121.

K'ang-hsi Emperor, *see under* Emperors of China.
Kalmuks, 59-60, 147, 164.
Kalons, 17, 46, 104, 133.
Kansu Province, 3.
Kashmir, 3, 34, 60-61, 164.
Kashmiris, 41, 46, 57, 61, 114, 163 n. 8, 164.
katas, 57, 57-58 n. 20, 59.
Kham, 12 n. 33.
Khatmandu, 23, 25, 108, 109 n. 41, 124 n. 17, 125, 128, 130-31.
Khubilai Khan, 10, 11, 13-14.
Kinloch, Captain, 23, 25, 27, 56 (n. 11).
Kirkpatrick, Captain, William, viii, 108-9, 130, 136-37.
Kirung, 114, 119.
Kokonor, 3, 58, 69, 123.
knives and cutlery, 58, 163.
Kuch Behar, *see* Cooch Behar.
Kumbum, 69, 71 n. 78.
Kuti, 115.

Ladakh, 3, 5, 42, 55 n. 5, 164.
Lalitavajra, 49 n. 86.
lamas (Tibetan monks), 9, 14, 55, 121-22.
Lamaism (Tibetan Buddhism), 7-12, 60, 111 n. 49, (112).
Latsan Khan, 15-16.
lead, 98.
leather, 30, 60, 164.
Lee, Wei Kuo, 89 n. 29.
Lévi, Sylvain, 22 notes 80 and 82, 131 n. 41.
Lhasa, 5, 11 n. 33, 15-17, 24, 32, 34, 37, 39, 40, 45-47, 50-51, 52-53, 61, 76, 87, 94, 98, 104, 106, 109, 119, 126, 134, 141, 150.
Lobzang Paldan Yeshes, *see* Panchen Lama, the Sixth.
Lobzang Tsering, 24.
Logan, James, Surgeon, 23, 25.
London, 25, 57.
Ludwig, Ernest, 15 n. 46.

Macartney, Lord George, 76-77, 102, 137-39, 142.
McDowell, D. H., 114, 125.

Macpherson, John, 102-3, 105-6, 115 n. 59.
Mahendra Malla, Rajah, 108.
Mahomed Rejeb, 114.
Mahomed Walli, 114.
Mahrattas, 116 n. 60.
Manchus, 12-16, 17 n. 56, 22, 36, 50-51, 87, 122, 123, 146, 149, 151.
Manchu language, 127-28.
Manichaeism, 7.
Marco Polo, 14.
Marici, the goddess, 122.
Markham, Sir Clements, viii, 31 n. 22, 35, 123 n. 14.
Marques, Fr. Manuel, 19.
mercury, 99, 162.
mines, 55-56, 97-98, 148, 163 n. 7.
minerals, 55-57, 162-64; *see also* gold, silver, lead, cinnabar, etc.
Ming Dynasty, 14, 57.
Moghuls, 24, 36, 116 n. 60, 157, n. 2.
Moghul Emperor, 139-40; Shah Alam, 115, 116 n. 60.
Mongol Dynasty, *see* Yüan Dynasty.
Mongolia (or "Tartary"), 4, 12, 15, 57, 64, 68, 80, 88, 133, 136, 149.
Mongolian language, 92 n. 45.
Mongols, 10, 13-16, 59-60, 63, 77, 86, 121; *see also* Buriats, Daghors, Kalmuks, Oelots, Tumets.
Monson, George, 64, 65.
Montgomerie, Colonel, 20 n. 75.
Moslems, 9, 19, 114, 125 n. 19.
Mukden, 12.
Mukwanpur, 128.
musical instruments, 120, 162.
musk, 31, 55, 63, 97, 99, 162, 164.
Mysore War, the Second, 107, 126.

Nawakot, 130, 131 n. 41.
Nepal, 3, 6, 22-24, 25, 27, 33 n. 28, 37, 38-39, 46, 48, 56, 61, 62, 75-76, 99, 108-13, 114 n. 56, 115, 119, 120, 130-31, 132, 136-37, 144, 148-49, 150, 162-63.
Nestorian Christianity, 7.
Newaris, 22-23, (25), 62, 108-9, 110.
Nilam, 114, 119.
Nomun Khan, 73 n. 82, 92 n. 45.

öbös, 132.
Odoric of Pordenone, 18 n. 65.
Oelots, 11, 15-16.
O-hui, 120, (122).

Pa-chung, 120, 122.
Padma (Paima), 30, (33), 41.
Padma Sambhava, 7, 8, 55-56.
Paima, *see* Padma.
Panchen Lamas, 11-12, 57, 121, 133, 149; the Fourth, 11; the Sixth, (13), 18, 24, 27-32, 36-37, 40-41, 42-46, 47, 48-52, 53, 57, 62, 66-69, 70-80, 82, 86, 88, 91 n. 37, 92, 93, 94, 104, 111-12, 146, 157-59; the Seventh, 82, 83, 86, 87, 89, 90-91, 93, 95, 103-4, 114-17, 121, 128, 129, 130, 133, 135, 139, 140 n. 72, 164.
Pao-t'ai, Amban, 121.
Patan, 108, 109 n. 41.
Pathans, 36.
Patna, 92, 136.
pearls, 58, 60, 63, 162, 163.
Peking, 12-13, 20, 36, 50, 67, 68, 69-70, 72, 74, 76, 78, 79, 82, 86, 94, 120, 122-23, 131, 132, 137, 139, 142, 146; Grand Lama of, *see* Changkya Hutukhtu.
Pelliot, Paul, 79 n. 99.
Persian language, 114, 128, 157 n. 2, 159 n. 3.
Phari Jong, 47, 132 n. 46, 142.
p'i-lêng, 140-41.
porcelain, 58, 162.
Portuguese, 19, 21, 68 n. 65.
Potala palace, 11, 16.
potatoes, 34 n. 31.
Pratap Singh Sahi, *see* Gurkha Rajahs.
precious stones, 32, 59 n. 26, 162, 163.
Pritchard, Earl H., 139 n. 70.
Prithvi Narayan, *see* Gurkha Rajahs.
Purangir, 30, (35), 36-37, 40, 42, 48, 57 n. 19, 62 n. 36, 66, 69-74, 79, 82, 103-6, 118, 127, 141, 142, 145-46.
Putte, Samuel van de, 20.

quicksilver, 99, 162.

Rajendra Vikram Sahi, *see* Gurkha Rajahs.
Rana Bahadur Sahi, *see* Gurkha Rajahs.
Rangpur, 40, 41, 80-81, 84, 92, 114, 156, 160, 164.
Ranjit Malla, Rajah, 109.
Red Cap lamas, 10, 11, 111 n. 49, 112.
Regent of Lhasa, the "old," 40, 44-47, 50-51; the "new," 80, 87, 92-93, 104.
Regent of Nepal, The, *see* Bahadur Sahi.
Regent of Tashilhunpo, The, *see* Chungpa Hutukhtu.
rhinoceros horns, 59 n. 26, 131.
rhubarb, 32.
rice, 57, 62, 163, 164.
Rockhill, W. W., 12-13, 14 n. 44, 69 n. 71, 113 n. 51.
Rolpahi Dorje, 49 n. 86.
Russia, 53 n. 100, 59-60, 88-89, 146-47, 164.

Sa-kya Sect, 10, 13.
salt, 55, 62, 99, 113, 162, 164.
Sandburg, Graham, 19 n. 71, 29 n. 10, 30 n. 15, 31 n. 22, 50 n. 90, 83 n. 4, 85 n. 12.
Sarat Chandra Das, *see* Das, Sarat Chandra.
Saunders, Robert, 81 n. 102, 83, 85, 90, 91.
seals of office, 10, 132 n. 45.
Shah Alam, *see* Moghul Emperor.
Shamarpa Hutukhtu, 75, 78, 111, 112-13, 119, 131, 133.
shawl goats, 33, 61, 84 n. 11, 164.
Shigatse, 19, 51 n. 92, 95, 121.
Siberia, 34, 60, (164).
Sikang, 3, 11 n. 33.
Sikkim, 3, 51-52, 108, 127, 132, 149-50.
silk, 30, 57-58, 59, 60, 100, 162.
silver, 30, 32, 34, 56, 58, 59, 60, 97-99, 100, 105 n. 18, 108-10, 119-20, 133, 162.

Sining, 58-59, 60, 61, 100, 123.
smallpox, 37, 42, 45, 69, 76, 80.
Solon tribe, 123.
Solpön Chenpo, The, 42, 73, (79), 82, 86, 87, 88, 103, 141.
Song-tsan Gam-po, King of Tibet, 5-6.
spices, 57, 60, 62, 90, 163.
Staunton, Sir George, Bart., 76-78, 109 n. 41, 112, 125, 142 n. 79.
Sun Shih-i, 141.
Sung Dynasty, 13.
Suryagiri (another name for Purangir), 140 n. 72.
Szechuan Province, 3, 15, 17, 58, 123, 124.

Tachienlu, 15, 17, 58.
T'ang Dynasty, 5-6, 10, 13.
Tangun horses, 160.
Taoism, 8 n. 18.
Tartars, see Mongols.
Tartary, see Mongolia.
Tashi Lama, see Panchen Lamas, and 27 n. 2.
Tashichu Jong (Tassisudon), 40 n. 50.
Tashilhunpo, 11, 23, 24, 27 n. 2, 30-31, 32, 36, 42, 43, 51-52, 53, 62, 66, 69, 72-74, 79, 80, 82, 85-89, 91, 92-96, 98, 99, 103-6, 112, 113 n. 54, 121-22, 124, 125, 133, 142, 164.
Tashilhunpo Temple, in Jehol, 78.
Tassisudon (Tashichu Jong), 40-41, 44, 45, 52, 85.
tea, 39, 57, 58, 59, 62, 100, 147, 162, 164.
Terpaling, 90, 104.
Teshoo Lama, see Panchen Lamas, and 27 n. 2.
Thok Jalung goldfields, 55.
Thunderbolt Sow, The, see Dorje Phagmo.
Tibet, 3-5, 9-22, 23, 24, 25, 26, 28, 29, 30-31, 32-35, 36, 37, 39, 41-53, 54-64, 67, 70, 74, 75-76, 78-79, 80, 85-91, 92-100, 103-6, 107-10, 113-14, 118, 119-20, 121-24, 131-34, 136-37, 142, 144-45, 146-47, 148-51; Eastern, 15, 17, 123, 133, see also Kham; Further, 17, 18, 19, 75,

111, 112, 121, 141, 145; Western, 19; the closing of, 36, 131-32, 141-43, 144-49.
Tibetan language, 7, 14, 78.
tobacco, 57, 58, 59, 162, 163-64.
trade and commerce, 21-22, 23-26, 29, 32-34, 39, 41, 43-44, 46-53, 54-64, 67, 82-85, 88, 91, 93-100, 104-6, 108, 110, 117-19, 124-25, 127, 130, 136-37, 144-49, 151, 162-64; see also gold, coral, silk, tea, etc.
tribute (to China), 14, 57, 58-59, 120, 121, 131, 142.
Tsaparang, 19.
Tsong Ka-pa, 10.
Tumets, 10.
Turkestan, 6, 15, 59, 80.
Turner, Captain Samuel, viii, 30 n. 18, 31, 33, 70 n. 74, 72, 73 n. 81, 74 notes 87 and 88, 83-100, 102, 103-4, 106, 108 n. 37, 109, 110, 112, 123 n. 14, 142, 145-48, 157 n. 1, 162-64.

Urga, 49 n. 86, 88; Grand Lama of, see Jebtsun Dampa Hutukhtu.

van de Putte, Samuel, see Putte, Samuel van de.
Verelst, Harry, Governor, 23 n. 84, 25.

Waddell, L. A., 6 n. 8, 28 n. 11.
Wên-ch'êng, Princess, 6.
wool, 31, 55, 61, 62, 162.

yaks and yaktails, 33, 34 n. 30, 55, 63, 84 n. 11.
Yangtze River, 55.
Yellow Cap lamas (Gelug-pa), 10, 11, 15, 111 n. 48.
Yellow River, 55.
Younghusband, Sir Francis, 28 n. 6, 147, 150-51.
Younghusband Expedition, 88, 147.
Yüan (or Mongol) Dynasty, 10, 13-14.
Yule, Colonel Henry, 14 n. 40.
Yunnan Province, 3, 17.
Yutog, Depön of, 119.